KETO SO COOKBOOK FOR BEGINNERS

EASY AND DELICIOUS SOUPS FOR YOUR LOW-CARB HIGH-FAT DIET

Copyright © 2018 by Shark publications

SHARK PUBLICATIONS

Copyright@Shark Publications 2018

All Rights Reserved

No part of this publication may be reproduced,

transmitted or stored in a retrieval system, in any form or by any means,

without permission in writing from Shark Publications.

This book is sold subject to the condition that it shall not,

by way of trade or otherwise, be lent, resold, hired out or otherwise circulated

without the Publisher's prior consent in any form of binding or cover,

other than that in which it is published.

KETO SOUPS COOKBOOK

WHY I WROTE THIS BOOK

Keto Recipies.

CHAPTER-1

Keto diet

CHAPTER 2

Different types of ketogenic diets

CHAPTER 3

Benefits of ketogenic diet

CHAPTER 4

GROCCERY LIST

CHAPTER 5

MACROS

CHAPTER 6

KICK START KETO

CHAPTER 7

10 Signs and Symptoms That You're in Ketosis

CHAPTER 8

KETO FLU

CHAPTER 9:

SIDE EFFECTS OF KETO DIET

CHAPTER 10

REMEDIES

1. Roasted Butternut Squash Soup
2. Keto instant pot chicken soup
3. Keto Chicken Enchilada Soup
4. Bacon Cauliflower Chowder
5. Avocado Chipotle Soup
6. Homemade Thai chicken soup
7. Hamburger stew
8. Broccoli cheese soup
9. Keto chicken ramen soup
10. Tomato basil soup
11. Keto Paleo Cabbage Roll Soup
12. Chicken kale soup
13. Greek Lemon Chicken Soup
14. Keto Soup with Sausage, Peppers, and Spinach
15. Pressure Electric Cooker pot chili
16. Pressure Electric Cooker pot vegetarian chili
17. Beef stew
18. Italian meatball soup
19. Low carb chili
20. Spanish / Mexican soup
21. Spinach soup
22 Cheesy cream of cauliflower soup
23. Creamy leek and salmon soup
24. Creamy Garlic Chicken Soup

25. Ham and Green Bean Soup
26. Coconut soup with shrimp or chicken
27. Spicy Cauliflower Soup
28. Sopa De Lima
29. Easy Green Chicken Enchilada Soup
30. Chile Relleno chicken soup
31. Keto-Bacon Cheeseburger Soup
32. Pork and Tomato Soup
34. Instant chicken fajita soup
35. Turkey soup, kale and pumpkin
36. Thai Tom Saap Pork Chop Soup
37. Creamy Soup with Cauliflower and Keto Ham
38. Bacon Stew
39. Asian Noodle Soup
40. Turkey and Butternut Soup with Ginger and Turmeric
41. Chilli with White Turkey and Light
42. Thai Beef and Broccoli Soup
43. Good Ole South Soup
44. Chile with low Carbohydrate Beans
45. Asian Soup with Keto Chicken Meatballs
46. Broccoli soup

About Author

ONE LAST THING

WHY I WROTE THIS BOOK

I wrote this book so that I can share the knowledge of Ketogenic diet with everyone who wants to lose weight and live a healthy lifestyle. This book will help you understand principles of ketogenic diet and how your body acts in keto state. There are so many myths and doubts related to Ketogenic diet, all doubts will be resolved in this book.

This book will give you complete information about the followings-

What is ketogenic diet?

Different types of ketogenic diets.

Benefits of ketogenic diet.

What to eat on ketogenic diet.

Getting started with Ketogenic diet.

How to reach Ketosis.

How to know if you have achieved ketosis.

Ketogenic diet Macros.

Dangers of Ketogenic diet.

Keto Flu.

Keto Recipies.

CHAPTER-1

Keto diet

Introduction

With the recent rave on internet, almost everyone is keen on getting fit; sometimes this could be a decision made on their own, other times it could be a decision influenced by external influences. Everyone these days wants to look fit, and even if you are not so enthusiastic about it, you visit social media platforms, see people post their photos and feel as though you are missing out on something.

In most ways, this rave for staying fit has proved beneficial, because it has made everyone become conscious about how healthy their lifestyle is and to take actionable steps to ensure that one stays and remain fit/healthy.

People ensure they stay fit by employing different method: some choose to burn it out by combining a healthy eating habit and working out; some chose to stay fit by sticking to healthy eating alone and leaving out the stressful workouts because it may be overwhelming to them that they can't keep up. Keto diet is one fine method employed by individuals to guarantee fitness.

There are different dieting plans that are employed by people keen on weight loss or looking for fitness and one popular diet plan employed by many, and is even recommended by health professionals is Keto Diet. The success rate recorded by those that have tried this plan has made it one of the most preferred dieting option for weight loss.

What is Keto Diet

I am pretty sure one way or the other you may have come across the phrase "Keto Diet" but you may not be so well informed about what it actually entails. I would be considered a peddler of half-baked knowledge if I try to explain what keto diet entails without enlightening you on some of the terminologies affiliated to it. Here are few of them:

Ketones: Without trying to sound too scientific, I would say, ketones in plain English are the major byproduct of fats broken down in the body.

Ketosis: This can be simply defined as a state where the body tissues experience an elevated level of ketones.

Ketogenesis: This is the biological process involved in breakdown of fats into ketones. Ketogenesis is an alternative biochemical process used by the body to produce energy when the primary biochemical process – like: glycolysis – is not being used.

Primarily, the body uses the process involved in the breakdown of glucose to produce energy needed for its inherent biochemical activities but on some certain conditions – like: during fasting, diabetes, or elevated fat reserve – the body instead uses this alternative pathway to produce energy.

I know, I said I would try not to go all scientific, but it is key to know the basics before we go all in into understanding how Keto Diet works.

Keto diet particularly is a meal plan that stresses on having more fatty foods, less carbohydrates and a moderate amount of protein. This meal plan exploits the understanding of how ketones are produced, and forces the body to move in the direction of using more fats– which is a consequence of a low carb diet.

The Chemistry Behind It:

Even if you have no scientific background, you must have heard that glucose is the primary energy co-efficient used by body tissues: muscles, brain etc. This explains why most athletes are given synthesized glucose (the white, crystallized substance normally packaged in a container) to replenish their energy – it is like the fastest go-to option for energy replenishment.

High carb diet means more production of glucose in the body (since it is a byproduct when broken down). When glucose becomes surplus in the blood, it is distributed to different metabolic pathways, one of them is *gluconeogenesis.*

On specific conditions like fasting, the body uses up the reserves to yield energy and when it has completely used up the glycogen reserve (with the help of glucagon) it goes ahead to use the fat reserves too, which ends up producing another energy coefficient known as *ketones*. This could also be the case for diabetic patients, because they have a particular constraint when it comes to synthesizing insulin, they summarily end up using mostly the fat reserves for the production of energy needed.

Now when you are on a keto diet, you are forcing the body to use the alternative means of producing energy, which is by production of Ketones. The diet therefore composes of high fatty foods and less carbs. This makes so much sense because when you eat less carbs, you have low glucose reserve and when the glucose reserve is low, the body is forced to seek an alternative means of producing energy. And since there is a high concentration of fatty foods, it is only natural that it opts for breaking it down to ketones which can be used as an energy co-efficient.

This is an attempt to explain its chemistry in the plainest English possible, without confusing you by juxtaposing too much scientific languages. I hope it makes sense to you.

So, how did we get here, using fats for fat loss?

Well, we have come a long way in the world of nutrition and are debating macros right from the start - especially carbohydrates and fats because they are linked to weight loss. Both have been demonized, celebrated and researched in every way possible.

But what does the research say?

It is becoming increasingly clear that the argument for choosing a low carbohydrate diet might be to try to reduce calories and lose weight. And while science is by no means conclusive and the best nutritional approaches can vary widely from human to human, we are seeing more and more people succeed in manipulating carbohydrates.

In short, the keto diet is the lowest carb diet we have - an intake of only 50-70 grams of carbs or less per day. Keto also requires a higher fat intake. In fact, most of your calories come from fats in keto diet. This combined macro approach allows your body to switch to fats (called ketosis) as the main source of fuel.

Ketosis is a proven phenomenon, but we are still discovering how beneficial it is, especially to lose weight. Let's see what we know.

Keto diet: trend or based on science

With the current keto trend, no one can deny that the ketogenic meal plan is an upward trend. But does that mean it's not based on science? Not necessarily.

Although almost all types of diets with the right micronutrients and calorie control can be healthy and effective, some studies show a specific benefit of low carbohydrate intake for weight loss and reduced cardiovascular disease.

But what about ketosis? This makes the keto diet unique, right?

The idea is that in the state of ketosis, the body can promote faster weight loss by actively burning fat as fuel.

But the past has taught us that the human body is complex - and theories often do not work the same when applied objectively to humans. That's why you can hear many health professionals refer to studies and discuss them. That's why it's so important to base our professional recommendations and decisions on the best studies we have, a practice known as evidence-based medicine and nutrition.

Are there any signs of ketosis promoting weight loss and overall health? Early studies indicate that this could be the case. However, there is still no good evidence that the ketogenic diet is superior to other low carbohydrate diets for weight loss.

Ketogenic diet results

An effective keto diet can yield many positive results. However, it depends on the results you are looking for to determine if this plan is right for you or not.

In particular, the keto diet appears to promote effective weight loss, improve glycemic control in diabetic patients, and helps to reduce cholesterol and improve blood pressure.

However, it may not be ideal for people with intense physical activity, such as for athletes - or for people who wants to develop muscles.

As with any diet, the results depend on if you do it the correct way.

Keto VS Other low carb diets

The difference between keto diet and traditional low carb diets such as Paleo, Atkins and South Beach lies mainly in ketosis - which has a lot to do with overall macro balance. In simple terms, the main difference is you have to consume even less carbohydrates while being on keto diet.

A healthy and balanced diet, recommended in the USDA's dietary guidelines, suggests a carbohydrate intake of 45 to 65 percent of your calories or about 250 grams of carbohydrate a day for a 2,000-calorie diet.

Low carb diets usually recommend half this amount, about 150 grams of carbs or less per day. Ketogenic diet further reduces this amount and recommends less than 50-70 grams of carbohydrates a day.

In addition, many low carbohydrate diets replace carbohydrates with higher protein intake. However, since too many proteins affect the functioning of ketosis, a keto diet suggests only a moderate protein value and focuses primarily on higher fat intake, which accounts for nearly 70% of the intake.

Carbohydrates: are they really so bad?

Understanding carbohydrates can seem complicated. Probably because we cannot agree on how many we need in our diet, what are the best sources of carbohydrates, or if we need them at all. We have seen that the right types of carbohydrates can be very beneficial to your body and are included in many successful weight loss diets. But there are also many low carbohydrate diets that seem to give promising results.

The argument against including too many carbohydrates include their effect on blood sugar, storage of insulin and fats, as well as a simple source of calories. But what exactly are carbohydrates and what do they do when you eat them?

Are carbohydrates and sugars the same?

Yes, sugar is a carbohydrate. And it is common for all carbohydrates to be called "sugars". But not all carbohydrates are equal, and that does not mean that the body equates all carbohydrates equal to table sugar. Some carbohydrates are very nutritious and can be exceptionally healthy for consumption.

This macro-group also includes fiber and complex starches, which are digested differently from conventional table sugar. Natural carbohydrates in foods that have many health benefits, such as fruits, beans, and dairy products, are not the same types of refined and processed sugars that are added to many foods.

What is glucose?

When you eat carbohydrates, they are broken down into a form of usable energy, glucose. As glucose circulates in your blood, it fuels your muscles with energy needed for your workout. Glucose is either used for instant energy, added to blood to regulate blood sugar, or stored in muscles, liver or fat cells for later use.

Do carbohydrates make you fat?

Insulin is needed to store glucose. Therefore, it makes sense that you release a surge of insulin after eating. Insulin helps to collect glucose and transmit it to your cells for storage. As this process stores glucose in fat cells, it is often mistaken for gaining body fat. It is also important to note that this insulin response is also necessary for muscle growth.

But eating carbohydrates alone will not let you gain weight or body fat. In fact, under normal circumstances, dietary fats are much more likely to be stored as fats than any other macro, especially when you consume more calories than you burn. Most people tolerate 100 to 500 g of carbohydrate a day without significantly contributing to fat storage. It has been shown that weight gain occurs when caloric intake exceeds caloric requirements.

Some people may think that diet-related weight loss can also help reduce energy or cause your body to burn more energy to digest the calories you consume. Your body is amazing in compromising and adapting. It is therefore difficult to take a single bodily process - such as extracting glucose for energy – and to assume that it is the only determining factor. In other words, metabolizing food is just not so easy. Changing a thing often causes a series of chain reactions in your body.

Can you survive on a diet without carbs?

Glucose is not only important for fast energy; it is also the only source of fuel able to cross the blood-brain barrier. In other words, your brain loves carbohydrates. This is another reason why your body prefers this macro for energy. Since glucose is the type of sugar in your blood, it is clearly important to maintain blood glucose control.

So what happens if you do not eat carbohydrates?

You will find another way! Carbohydrates may be the easiest way to get glucose, but it's not the only option.

How your body produces glucose without carbohydrates

Without carbohydrates, your body needs to find other ways to recover glucose or find another form of energy that is usable, effective, and able to fuel your brain. Your glucose storage capacity is limited and you can become carb depleted fairly quickly. When this happens, your body starts by using dietary proteins or stored proteins (aka your muscles) and lipids to produce glucose through a process called gluconeogenesis.

Proteins are not a desirable source for substitution of glucose because their main function is to build and maintain all body cells (including precious muscles). This process is important and cannot be replaced by other macros. For this reason, the protein is the only macro with a recommended minimum intake. So, if carbohydrates intake is not high, you need to find other ways to meet your energy needs. This is where fat comes into play.

Fat is important for storing essential nutrients, plays an important role in the regulation of hormones and serves as a cushion for your organs and your entire body. Unlike carbohydrates, your body store fats very well. For a variety of reasons, fat is a preferred source of energy storage, in addition to its almost unlimited capacity.

Fats are also high in calories, delivering twice as much calories or twice as much energy as carbohydrates and proteins. This makes it a pretty efficient fuel source when you need it. Fats are sustainable source of energy for survival - you can live on your fat reserves longer than your muscles or carbohydrate stores.

Where ketones come in

Ketones are produced by a process called ketogenesis when the demand for fatty acids as fuel increases - or when the source of glucose becomes limited. As your body produces more ketones, you enter a condition called ketosis. Glucose no longer remains the main fuel source for daily energy needs: ketones are!

Ketones act as a quick source of energy when needed, and can also provide your brain with the fuel needed to function. Since this process exists, carbohydrates are not necessarily vital nutrients for survival. And it is possible to live off a diet without carbohydrates.

Ketones as fuel

Any living animal can switch from glucose to ketones for fuel. Then why does not our body do it all the time?

Because ketones are not the preferred source of energy for body organs when carbohydrates are available.

Fats as fuel

Even if you consume lots of carbohydrates in your diet, you can still use fats as a source of energy. The type of fats you use comes mainly from stored fats (fatty acids). Stored fats are actually a preferred source of energy between meals, during rest and after a long workout.

Your body has an almost unlimited capacity to store and use fats when compared to carbohydrates. Using fat gives you twice as much energy (one gram of fat equals 9 calories, whether you eat it or burn it), compared to carbohydrates that only deliver 4 calories per gram.

Ketones as fuel

Ketones are formed when there are insufficient carbohydrates or insufficient glucose in your body. Although ketones can be used as stored fats, they are different from conventional fatty acids because ketones can be used as a quick source of fuel, and brain energy source instead of glucose. In other words, ketones replace glucose with fatty acids in your body.

For dietary purposes, ketosis can be achieved in two ways:

1. In a state of pure starvation - who wants that?

2. Extreme restriction of carbohydrates

Ketones supplements can also be used. Although there is not enough evidence to support their effectiveness in accelerating ketosis or supporting athletic performance, some studies suggest that they could promote the use of ketones as fuel even when one is not following ketogenic diet. However, this is different from eating a low carbohydrate diet because ketone supplements do not require ketosis and theoretically are a faster way to gain energy.

CHAPTER 2

Different types of ketogenic diets

There are three types of ketogenic diet, each one is little different from another. Test all and see which suits you the best.

Standard Ketogenic diet

This is the most popular type of ketogenic diet. This diet is high in fats, moderate in proteins and very low in carbohydrates. This diet is best for those who do really low intensity activities.

In this diet you are allowed to consume really low amount of carbohydrates generally around 20-70 grams. If you consume more than 70 grams of carbohydrates per day, then you might get out of ketosis.

Carbohydrate limits are different for different people, but the general approach is to avoid breads, pastas, fruits (high in carbohydrates) and everything that includes high amount of carbohydrates.

You are allowed to have green vegetables, seeds, nuts which are low in carbohydrates, on this diet; they will be the primary source of carbohydrates that you will consume in Standard Ketogenic diet.

Targeted Ketogenic diet

In targeted ketogenic diet you consume carbohydrates around your workouts; usually 30-60 minutes before a workout, so that your workouts performance do not go down and high intensity exercises are performed effectively and efficiently. Rest of the time you follow standard ketogenic diet. This diet helps in promotion of glycogen replenishment.

Targeted Ketogenic diet will be best suited for these individuals:

1. Athletes that need carbohydrates to improve their exercise performance.

2. People who are new to exercise programme.

Cyclical Ketogenic diet

Cyclical ketogenic diet combines carbohydrates loading days and standard ketogenic diet. This diet is best suited for those who perform really heavy workouts and high intensity trainings. This diet is for athletes and bodybuilders, since high intensity is required in their workouts and their performance should not suffer with ketogenic diet. They do require carbohydrates to maintain high quality workouts.

They are allowed to have carbohydrates to replenish themselves once or twice a week, so that they get the fuel for their trainings.

Cyclical ketogenic diet is not like targeted ketogenic diet, the main goal in targeted ketogenic diet is to keep blood sugar and muscles glycogen at a moderate level. The goal of Cyclical Ketogenic diet is to completely replenish glycogen during fuel loading and to deplete glycogen and raise ketone levels between carbohydrate charges.

High-protein ketogenic diet: This is basically almost the same as the standard ketogenic diet, the only discrepancy being that you will have to incorporate more protein into the diet. So instead of the 20% protein that is expected to be ingested in the standard ketogenic diet, in this case, you are expected to ingest 35% protein while the fat concentration reduces to 60% and the quantity of the carbs expected to be eaten remains 5%.

This plan also proves beneficial because research has shown that protein aids in weight loss; one of the widely acclaimed reasons for the claim is that protein rich foods are more filling than carbohydrates– which means that you will end up eating less calories than you would on high carbohydrate diet.

Calorie-restricted ketogenic diet: This is almost the same as the standard ketogenic diet, what sets it apart from standard ketogenic diet is that the calorie intake is restricted to a certain amount. Although most scientists argue that whether the calorie intake is being checked or not, the keto diet would still be successful if followed correctly.

One of the benefits of calorie-restricted ketogenic diet is that it is very helpful for cancer patients to help control the growth of tumor; the concept being that cancer cells only employ lactate and glucose to grow but not ketones. If you want to read further on this, you can visit any of the following links:

https://www.ncbi.nlm.nih.gov/pmc/articles/PMC4215472/,
https://nutritionandmetabolism.biomedcentral.com/articles/10.1186/1743-7075-4-5.
https://www.researchgate.net/profile/Linda_Nebeling/publication/15407903_Effects_of_a_Ketogenic_Diet_on_Tumor_Metabolism_and_Nutritional_Status_in_Pediatric_Oncology_Patients_Two_Case_Reports/links/0fcfd50c8978caedb1000000.pdf
http://pediatrics.aappublications.org/content/119/3/535.

Medium-chain-triglycerides Ketogenic Diet: This keto diet maintains the same specifics particular to the standard ketogenic diet, the only difference is that, in this case, the fat content of the diet are most preferred to come from a particular type of fats which are known as Medium chain triglycerides.

The interesting thing about this diet is that, you can eat more proteins and carbs while still trying to maintain Ketosis; an explanation for this is that, medium chain triglycerides have a higher conversion rate to ketones than the long-chain triglycerides you would find in normal dietary fat.

A major concern about this type of fat is that if taken too much, it could make the body susceptible to stomach upset and diarrhea. One way to prevent this is to balance the MCT fat to non-MCT fat. One common MCT source you can find anywhere is coconut oil.

All ketogenic diets discussed in this chapter are equally effective and important, none holds more credence over the others, don't allow anyone tell you otherwise. All you have to do is pick the one that is most convenient for you and ensure strict adherence to it to yield positive results. I believe in due time, and with consistency, you will end up seeing positive results.

CHAPTER 3

Benefits of ketogenic diet

Ketogenic diet is more than just a diet, it is a lifestyle. When you hear people say Ketogenic diet changed their lives forever, they are not kidding; they really mean it.

Weight loss

Ketogenic diet is the best diet available in the market. With ketogenic diet your fat loss happens really quickly and in a healthy manner because your body is using your own fat reserves for energy even while doing your mundane tasks. You don't feel hungry on this diet. Your body turns itself into a fat burning machine.

Blood sugar level

Diabetes is caused because your body is not able to handle high insulin levels. Ketogenic diet automatically lowers your blood sugar levels because you are not consuming carbohydrates which turn into glucose and increases your blood sugar stream.

Keto diet is really very helpful and effective for those suffering from diabetes.

Ketogenic diet controls your blood sugar levels and gives you more control in life.

Mental focus

Ketogenic diet gives you a laser sharp focus; you are not distracted with your thoughts. Your mental performance increases while being on ketogenic diet. Many people follow keto lifestyle just because they want to increase their mental focus and want to achieve success; they are perfectly fit but still follow this diet.

Ketones are really great fuel source for your brain and this is the reason why your mental performance increases while being on a Ketogenic diet. Increase of fatty acids really enhances your mental focus.

Increase in energy

As you already know that liver turns fats into energy source when you are following ketogenic diet, but do you know that while being on Ketogenic diet, your energy levels increases massively because your body which was running by glucose, needed constant supply of glucose but on ketosis your body functions using ketones which are more reliable sources of energy.

Better appetite control

When your body runs on glucose, you often find yourself hungry all the time but on Ketogenic diet your appetite is much more controlled and you don't feel hungry all the time because fats are naturally more satisfying and they end up leaving our body in satiated state for much longer. Now you can say goodbye to random cravings which you used to feel all the time being on a normal diet.

Epilepsy

Since 1900, Ketogenic diet is used to cure epilepsy. Today also it is the most common way to cure childrens suffering from epilepsy.

Cholesterol and blood pressure

Ketogenic diet improves your triglyceride levels and cholesterol levels. The benefit of this is that there is very less toxic build up in the arteries which allow blood to flow throughout the body as it should flow.

Ketogenic diet increases your HDL (good cholesterol) and decreases LDL (bad cholesterol).

According to various researches, it has been found that low carbohydrate diet improves your blood pressure.

Excess weight gain most often leads to blood pressure issues. With ketogenic diet you lose all your unwanted fat, so it naturally improves your blood pressure.

Insulin resistance

Type II diabetes is caused due to insulin resistance. Ketogenic diet naturally lowers insulin levels of an individual to healthy ranges, so that they are no longer in the group of people that are on the cusp of acquiring diabetes.

Acne

Ketogenic diet improves your skin too. A lot of people have experienced the benefit of a clear and healthy skin.

CHAPTER 4
GROCCERY LIST

Your Ultimate Keto Diet Grocery List

Shopping on keto diet can be little difficult. Many processed and packaged foods are not allowed, and some whole foods are too starchy (such as sweet potatoes). You need to fill your plate with low-carbohydrate and high-fat foods such as red meat, seafood, and good fats.

We asked nutritionists to find out what foods should be part of your keto eating plan. Following are the foods that you should buy.

1 Low carbohydrate vegetables

Some of the vegetables which are perfect for ketogenic diet are as following

1	Arugula
2	Spinach
3	Eggplant
4	Mushrooms
5	Broccoli
6	Cauliflower
7	Zucchini
8	Bell peppers
9	Fennel
10	Cabbage
11	Celery
12	Brussels
13	Sprouts
14	Kale

Low carb vegetables contain lots of fibers, vitamins, minerals, antioxidants and more

Some of the vegetables that should be avoided are as following –

1	Carrots,
2	Yams,
3	Beets,
4	Turnips,
5	Sweet potatoes
6	Plain potatoes

2. *Fruits with low sugar content*

Some of the fruits which are perfect for ketogenic diet are as following

1	Tomatoes
2	Avocados
3	Blackberries
4	Raspberries
5	Blueberries
6	Strawberries
7	Coconut
8	Lemon
9	Lime

Even when you consume very less carbohydrates and sugar, it is still possible to eat fruits on Keto diet.

Some of the fruits that should be avoided are as following –

1	Apples
2	Pears
3	Bananas
4	Pineapples
5	Papayas
6	Grapes
7	Fruit juices

3. Seafood

Some of the seafood's which are perfect for ketogenic diet are as following

1	Wild salmon
2	Sardines
3	Mackerel
4	Shrimp
5	Crab
6	Tuna
7	Mussels
8	Cod

The above options are an excellent source of healthy fats like omega-3 fatty acids as well as other beneficial nutrients like protein and selenium.

4. Meat, poultry and eggs

Some of the meats which are perfect for ketogenic diet are as following

1	Chicken
2	Turkey
3	Beef
4	Pork
5	Lamb
6	Eggs
7	Duck

Meat products are an important part of the keto diet, but experts emphasize the importance of choosing quality. "Because keto diets rely heavily on animal protein, it's important to buy organic poultry.

5. Nuts and seeds

Some of the nuts which are perfect for ketogenic diet are as following

1	Macadamia nuts
2	Flax seeds
3	Brazil nuts
4	Chia seeds
5	Walnuts
6	Pecans
7	Hemp seeds
8	Hazelnuts
9	Sesame seeds
10	Pumpkin seeds
11	Almonds

Nuts and seeds are the best snacks for keto diet. They are full of fats and proteins and help you stay full between meals.

6. Dairy products

Some of the dairy products which are perfect for ketogenic diet are as following

1	Cheese
2	Cottage cheese
3	Natural Greek yogurt
4	Cream
5	Butter

Dairy products are a good source of healthy fats, proteins and calcium.

7. Oils

Some of the oils which are perfect for ketogenic diet are as following

1	Extra virgin olive oil
2	Coconut oil
3	Avocado oil
4	Nut oil
5	Coconut butter
6	MCT oil

Oils, whether from fruits such as olives or nuts such as walnuts, are an excellent source of healthy fats. Since everyone has a unique taste, we recommend that you fill your pantry with a few different varieties.

8. Keto-approved condiments

Some of the condiments which are perfect for ketogenic diet are as following

1	Mayonnaise
2	Olive oil
3	Mustard
4	Unsweetened ketchup
5	Oil-based salad dressings

It can be difficult to find condiments that are keto friendly. If in doubt, check the nutritional information to make sure no sugar is added (this is especially important with ketchup, which can be a big sugar bomb).

9. Eggs

Like poultry and meat, eggs are another excellent source of animal protein and are among the most popular foods in keto.

10. Olives

Although technically olives are fruits, we believe that olives deserve a shout-out as they are also an excellent source of healthy fats and are one of the few keto-approved packaged foods. In addition, they are an excellent source of antioxidants, satisfy your cravings for something salty and have low carbohydrate content.

11. Keto-approved snacks

Some of the snacks which are accepted in ketogenic diet are as following

1	No-added sugar nut butter
2	Sugar-free jerky
3	Dried seaweed
4	Nuts
5	Low-carb crackers

Whole foods are always the best, but sometimes we understand that you simply need the convenience of a pre-packaged and bought snack in the store.

12 coffee and tea

Phew! Keto does not mean you have to give up your caffeine

13. Chocolates

"If you like chocolate, you can treat yourself, However, not all varieties are the same: Just check the label to make sure it contains at least 70% cocoa and contains less carbohydrate.

CHAPTER 5
MACROS

Macro is the short form of macronutrients (fats, proteins and carbohydrates). These macros are the basis of calories that you consume.

Calculating your macronutrients and total calories is very important on Ketogenic diet. First calculating macros will look really tough, but it is actually really easy once you understand it.

Everyone is different so macros are different for everyone. Total calories are different for everyone. Those who live really active lifestyle will need more calories than those who don't work out at all.

When calculating macros, the first step is to calculate your TDEE (Total Daily Energy Expenditure). It is basically total number of calories that you burn in a day. If you eat less than your total daily energy expenditure then you will lose weight, but if you eat more than your total daily energy expenditure then you will gain weight.

BASIC FORMULA

In this formula first we will calculate your energy expenditure when you are resting, that is energy required to run your body when you don't move at all.

For males

10 x weight (kg) + 6.24 x height (cm) – 5 x (age) + 6 = Resting energy expenditure.

For females

10 x weight (kg) + 6.24 x height (cm) – 5 x (age) – 159 = Resting energy expenditure.

Since most people do move and not just lie in their bed, next we have to find expenditure of their movements.

Sedentary

Walking, talking, eating etc. Normal day to day mundane activities. (REE x 1.1)

Light activity

Activities which burn around 200-400 calories for women and 250-500 calories for men come under light activity. (REE x 1.38)

Moderate activity

Activities which burns 400-650 calories for women and 500-800 calories for men comes under moderate activity. (REE x 1.6).

Very active

Activities which burn more than 651 calories for women and more than 801 calories for men comes under very active.(REE x 1.8).

A typical TDEE equation is like this

Let's say you are 30 years old, 184 cm, 90 kgs, very active man

These will be your results

(10 x weight (kg) + 6.24 x height (cm) – 5 x age (y) + 6 = REE) x 1.8 = TDEE

10 x 90 + 6.24 x 184 – 5 x 30 + 6 = REE

900 + 1148.16 – 150 + 6 = REE

1904.16 = REE

1904.16 x 1.8 = 3427.488

TDEE = 3427.488

If your Total daily energy expenditure is 3427.488.

If you will eat more than this, you will gain weight.

If you eat exactly 3427 calories than you will neither lose weight nor will you gain weight.

If you will eat less than 3427 calories then you will lose weight for sure.

Losing weight

If you want to lose weight then I will recommend don't drop your calories more than 20 % of your total daily energy expenditure. This way you will have enough energy to carry out your mundane tasks and live life with ease. You will stick to your diet but if you drop your calories too much than you will become demotivated and irritated by this diet and you will find yourself binge eating.

Gaining weight

Same goes with gaining weight, increase your calories by 20 %. This way you will gain lean muscles and will stay in control of your life.

MACROS

First step was getting your TDEE. Now we will calculate macronutrients that make up your diet.

1gram of protein = 4 calories.

1 gram of fat = 9 calories.

1 gram of carbohydrates = 4 calories.

So suppose you want to lose weight and your TDEE is 2000 calories per day.

You will consume around 1600 calories (2000 – 20 % of 2000).

FATS

Now 70 % of 1600 will be from fats.

70 % of 1600 = 1120.

1120 / 9 = 124 grams (1 gram of fats = 9 calories)

1120 Calories of fats means 124 grams of fats.

PROTEINS

25 % will be from proteins.

So 25 % of 1600 = 400 calories.

400/4 = 100 grams of proteins will be consumed.

CARBOHYDRATES

5% OF 1600 calories will be from carbohydrates which will be around 80 grams of carbohydrates. But try to lower your carbohydrate intake overtime; it should get below 50 grams per day.

CHAPTER 6
KICK START KETO

KICK START KETOSIS

1. Add coconut oil to your diet

Eating coconut oil can help you get into ketosis quickly. It contains fats called medium chain triglycerides (MCT).Unlike most fats, MCTs are rapidly absorbed and taken directly into the liver where they can be immediately used for energy or converted into ketones.

Infact, it has been suggested that coconut oil consumption is one of the best ways to increase ketone levels in people with Alzheimer's disease and other nervous system disorders, Although coconut oil contains four types of MCT,s, 50% of its fats come from lauric acid.

Some research suggests that fat sources containing high levels of lauric acid can produce a more sustained level of ketosis.
MCTs have been used to induce ketosis in epileptic children without limiting carbohydrates as drastically as the classic ketogenic diet.

If you add coconut oil to your diet, it is a good idea to do it slowly to minimize digestive side effects such as stomach cramps or diarrhea. Start with one teaspoon a day and work up to two or three tablespoons a day for one week. You can find coconut oil in your grocery or shop online.

2. Increase physical activity

. If you are more active, you can achieve ketosis more quickly. When you exercise, you take energy from glycogen stored in your body. These are usually replenished when you eat carbohydrates, which are broken down into glucose and then converted to glycogen.

However, when carbohydrate intake is minimized, glycogen levels remain low. In response, your liver increases the production of ketones, which can be used as an alternative fuel source for your muscles.

One study found that at low blood ketone concentrations, exercise increases the rate at which ketones are produced. However, when blood ketone levels are already high, they do not increase with exercise and may even decrease for a short time.

It has also been shown that fasting increases the ketone content. In a small study, nine older women exercised both before and after a meal. Their ketone levels in the blood were 137 to 314% higher when exercising before a meal compared to exercising after a meal.

Remember, although the body increases the production of ketones, it may take one to four weeks for your body to adjust fully to the use of ketones and fatty acids as the main fuel. During this time, physical performance may be temporarily reduced

3. Increase your healthy fat intake

Consuming a lot of healthy fats can increase your ketone levels and help you achieve ketosis. Ketogenic diet for weight loss, metabolic health and physical performance typically provide between 60% - 80% of the calories from fats.

The classic ketogenic diet which is used to treat epilepsy contains even more fats, usually between 85 and 90% of calories. However, an extremely high intake of fats does not necessarily lead to higher ketones.

A three-week study of 11 healthy people, we compared the effects with different amount of fats intake. Overall, ketone levels were similar in individuals who consumed 79% or 90% of calories from fats. Since fat is such an important part of a ketogenic diet, it is important to choose high quality fats.

Good fats are olive oil, avocado oil, coconut oil, butter, lard and tallow. However, if your goal is to lose weight, you should make sure that you do not consume too many calories as this can affect your weight loss.

4. *Try a Short Fast*

Another way to get into ketosis is to not eat for several hours. In fact, many people experience a slight ketosis between dinner and breakfast. Children with epilepsy may need to fast for 24 to 48 hours before starting a ketogenic diet. This is done to quickly penetrate the ketosis so that seizures can be reduced sooner.

Intermittent fasting, a dietary approach that involves regular short fasting, can also induce ketosis. In addition, "fasting" is another ketone-boosting approach.

5. *Make sure you have enough protein*

Achieving ketosis requires adequate but not excessive protein intake. The classic ketogenic diet used in epileptic patients contains very less carbohydrates and proteins to maximize ketone levels.

The same diet may also be beneficial for cancer patients as it may limit tumor growth. However, for most people it is not a healthy practice to reduce proteins to increase ketone production.

First, it is important to consume enough proteins to provide the liver with amino acids that can be used for gluconeogenesis, meaning "the production of new glucose."

In this process, your liver supplies glucose for the few cells and organs in your body that cannot use ketones as fuel, such as; your red blood cells and parts of the kidney and brain.

Second, protein intake should be sufficient to maintain muscle mass when carbohydrate intake is low, especially during weight loss.

Although weight loss usually results in both, muscle and fat loss, consuming sufficient amounts of protein in a low carbohydrate ketogenic diet can help maintain muscle mass.

In a study of 17 overweight men, a ketogenic diet that delivered 25-30% of the calories from proteins for four weeks resulted in an average of 1.52 mmol / L of blood ketone. This is well within the nutrient ketose range of 0.5-3.0 mmol / L.

6. Adjust your diet according to ketones level

Achieving and maintaining a ketosis condition depends on individuals. Since every one's body is different.

Therefore, it can be helpful to test your ketone levels to make sure you achieve your goals.

The three types of ketones - acetone, beta- hydroxybutyrate and acetoacetate - can be measured in breath, blood or urine.

Acetone is present in your breath, and studies have shown that testing acetone breath levels is a reliable method of monitoring acetone in individuals when they are following ketogenic diet.

The Ketonix meter measures acetone in your breath. Once you inhale the meter, a colour flashes to indicate that whether you are in ketosis or not and how high your level is. Ketones can also be measured with a blood ketone meter. A small drop of blood is deposited on a strip which gets inserted into the meter.

CHAPTER 7

10 Signs and Symptoms That You're in Ketosis

1. Bad breath

People often report bad breath when they achieve ketosis. It is actually a common side effect. Many people who follow ketogenic diet or similar diet, such as the Atkins diet, report that their breath smells weird.

This is due to high ketone content. The specific culprit is acetone, a ketone that exits the body through urine and breath.

2. Weight loss

The ketogenic diet as well as the normal low carbohydrate diet are very effective in losing weight. As dozens of weight loss studies have shown, you are more likely to lose weight in the short and long term if you switch to a ketogenic diet. A fast weight loss can occur in the first week. Although, it is mainly water.

3. Increased ketones in the blood

One of the properties of a ketogenic diet is lowering blood sugar levels and increasing ketones. When you switch to ketogenic diet, you start burning fat and using ketones as the main fuel.

The most reliable and accurate method of measuring ketosis is to measure your ketone levels in the blood with a special meter.

The measurement of ketones in your blood is the most accurate method of testing ketones and is used in majority of the research studies.

4. Increased ketones in the breath or urine

A respiratory analyzer is another method of measuring ketone levels in your blood.

It monitors acetone, one of the three main ketones present in the blood during ketosis.

This will give you an idea of how much ketone is in your body as more acetone leaves your body.

5. Suppression of appetite

Many people report a decrease in hunger on a ketogenic diet.

The reasons for this are still being investigated.

However, it has been suggested that this reduction in hunger is due to increased proteins and vegetables intake as well as changes in the body's hunger hormones.

Ketone themselves can also affect your brain to reduce your appetite.

6. Increased concentration and energy

People often report brain fog, fatigue, and discomfort at the beginning of a very low carbohydrate diet. This is referred to as "low carbohydrate flu" or "keto flu". However, long-term ketogenic dieters often report increased concentration and energy.

When you start a low-carbohydrate diet, your body needs to adjust itself to burn more fats than carbohydrates.

When you get into ketosis, a large part of the brain burns ketones instead of glucose. It may take few days or weeks for this to work properly.

7. Short-term fatigue

The initial switch to a ketogenic diet could be one of the main problems of the new regime. Well-known side effects include weakness and tiredness.

This often causes people to give up their diet before they become completely adapted to ketosis and have many long-term benefits.

These side effects are natural. After working with a carbohydrate fuel system for several decades, your body needs to adapt to a different system.

As you can imagine, this change does not happens overnight. It usually takes 7 to 30 days for ketosis to complete.

To reduce fatigue during this change, you can increase electrolytes intake.

8. Decrease in performance for short time

As mentioned earlier, the removal of carbohydrates at the beginning can cause general fatigue. This involves an initial decline in physical performance.

This is mainly due to the reduction in glycogen stores in your muscles, which is the most important and effective source for all forms of high intensity exercises.

After a few weeks, many ketogenic dieters report that their performance returns to normal.

9. Digestive problems

A ketogenic diet usually involves a big change in the type of foods you eat.

Digestive problems like constipation and diarrhea are common side effects in the beginning.

Some of these problems should be alleviated after the transitional period. However, it should be noted that various foods can cause digestive problems.

10. Insomnia

A big problem for many ketogenic dieters is sleep, especially when they change their diet for the first time.

Many people report insomnia when they drastically reduce their carbs. However, this usually improves within a few weeks.

Many long-term ketogenic dieters say they sleep better after adjusting to the diet compared to before starting ketogenic diet.

CHAPTER 8
KETO FLU

What is keto flu?

Keto flu is set of symptoms that some people may experience at the beginning of ketogenic diet.

These symptoms, which may resemble the flu, are caused when the body is trying to adjust to a new diet with very few carbohydrates.

Reducing carbohydrate consumption forces the body to burn ketones for energy instead of glucose.

This drastic reduction in carbohydrates can shock the body and lead to withdrawal symptoms, similar to those seen when an addictive substance such as caffeine is discontinued.

The signs of keto flu can occur in the first few days after reducing carbohydrates.

The symptoms can vary from mild to severe and from person to person.

While some people may switch to ketogenic diet without any side effects, others may experience one or more of the following symptoms:

Nausea
Vomiting
Constipation
Diarrhea
Headache
Irritability
Weakness
Muscle cramps
Dizziness
Poor concentration

Stomach pain
Muscle soreness
Insomnia
Sugar cravings

How can you get rid of the keto flu?

Keto flu can make you feel sick.

Fortunately, there are ways to reduce your flu symptoms and help your body to easily overcome the transition phase.

Stay hydrated

Drinking enough water is necessary for optimal health and may help to reduce the symptoms.

A keto diet can lead to a rapid loss of water supply and increase the risk of dehydration.

Glycogen, the stored form of carbs, holds the water in the body. When the carbohydrates are reduced from the diet, the glycogen level drops and water is eliminated from the body.

Being hydrated can help with symptoms such as tiredness and muscle cramps.

Avoid long workouts

Although exercise is important for staying healthy and maintaining weight, avoid difficult exercises when you experience keto-flu symptoms.

Fatigue, muscle spasms and upset stomach are common in the first week of a ketogenic diet. It may be a great idea to let the body rest.

Consume more electrolytes

Consumption of electrolytes in this diet can help to reduce the symptoms of keto-flu.

When you follow a ketogenic diet, your insulin levels drop.

As the level of insulin decreases, kidney releases excess sodium from the body.

In addition, the keto diet limits many potassium-rich foods, including fruits, beans and starchy vegetables.

Getting good amount of these important nutrients is a great way to control the adjustment phase of the diet.

Add salt to your food, including high-potassium, environmentally friendly foods such as green leafy vegetables and avocados, is a great way to maintain an electrolyte balance.

These foods are also rich in magnesium, which can relieve muscle spasms, sleep disorders, and headaches.

Sleep for 7-8 hours

Fatigue and irritability are common complaints in people who adapt to a ketogenic diet.

Lack of sleep leads to elevated cortisol levels, a stress hormone that can negatively affect mood and exacerbate the symptoms of keto flu.

Reduce Caffeine Consumption: Caffeine is a stimulant that can negatively impact sleep. If you drink caffeinated drinks, do so only in the morning so your sleep will not be affected.

Avoid Ambient Light: Turn off cell phone, computer and TV in the bedroom to create a dark environment and promote a good night's sleep.

Take a Bath: You can relax by adding Epsom salt or lavender essential oil to your bath.

Get up at the same time: Getting up at the same time each day can help improve your sleep quality over time.

How long will it last?

Fortunately, for most people, the unpleasant symptoms of keto flu last only about a week.

However, some people may find it more difficult to adapt to this high fat and low carbohydrate diet.

Fortunately, these symptoms gradually decrease as your body gets used to converting ketones into energy.

However, it is best to ask your doctor if you feel particularly bad and have symptoms such as persistent diarrhoea, fever, or vomiting.

Who should avoid ketogenic diet?

Although ketogenic diet may be useful for many people, it is not suitable for everyone.

For example, the ketogenic diet may not be suitable for children, adolescents and pregnant women unless it is used for therapeutic purposes under medical supervision.

This diet should be avoided by individuals suffering from certain diseases, such as kidney, liver or pancreatic diseases.

In addition, diabetics who wish to follow a ketogenic nutritional plan should consult their doctors to determine if this diet is safe and appropriate for their particular needs.

After all, this diet may not be suitable for people with cholesterol hypersensitivity.

CHAPTER 9:
SIDE EFFECTS OF KETO DIET

Like everything in life that promises desirable pros or advantages, there are inherent disadvantages to be worried about; even keto diet is not spared by this general principle.

The side effects of keto diet that will be discussed in this chapter is not an attempt to dissuade you from going keto, a much better way to look at them are **disclaimers** to keep you in check – this is to ensure that you are not caught unaware and to know what to expect as you go ahead with this dieting plan.

Here are few of the side effects to be worried about:

1. Ketoacidosis

This is a consequential situation that results from depending too much on fats as the primary energy source. What happens in this case is that as a result of increasing breakdown of fats, the concentration of ketones (which is the primary byproduct of this reaction) elevates, making the blood more acidic than it should be; this ends up posing a threat to the liver, kidney and brain.

Ideally, patients diagnosed with diabetes 1 & 2 are usually people who stand at higher risk of experiencing ketoacidosis, because the condition – diabetes mellitus – restricts them from metabolizing glucose efficiently; hence, depending on an alternative pathway to provide energy for proper functioning of body's organs – which is ketogenesis (a pathway where fats are broken down to glucose).

Ideally, I would advise diabetic patients to steer clear of keto diet or better still seek medical advice from a medical practitioner before proceeding with the diet.

A reasonable solution to this is engaging in a keto diet plan that allows for consumption of carbs on some days, nutritionists refer to this as carb cycling – a keto diet technique that employs the strategy of making room for "cheat days," which are days you allow your body to binge on high carb diet than the keto diet would normally permit. These days are normally set out to be once or twice in a week.

2. Nutrient deficiencies

In the debate between medical practitioners on whether keto dieting is healthy or not, this is one point that is always hammered on by the opposing side. They argue that subjecting oneself to a diet plan that almost eliminates the intake of carbs makes the individual lack some nutrients that are affiliated to high carb intake. The following are some of the nutrients that are argued to be lacking in those indulging in keto diet:

Fiber: you know as a result of going keto, the person is advised against eating high carb foods which also includes: high caloric fruits and starchy vegetables. Most fruits and vegetables known to have high caloric contents are also highly composed of fiber; this implies that, you not eating these foods which make your intake of fiber to be lower than it should be. And there are consequences that come with deficiency of fiber, one of them is dysfunctional bowel movement: this explains why some people experience diarrhea as they start the keto diet plan.

Potassium: Also, not taking high caloric fruits and vegetables can make your body's potassium concentration go lower than normal and this is considered unhealthy because potassium is a co-factor that is essential in a lot of metabolic reactions taking place in the body every day– protein biosynthesis, electrolyte balance, blood pressure control etc.

So not taking these fruits could make you susceptible to more harm than good. As a solution, dieticians advise those engaging in this diet plan to incorporate foods that are low in carb but highly rich in fiber and potassium like chia seeds and avocado respectively.

3. Change in breath

Most people I know experience a change in how their breath smells as they start to follow this diet plan strictly. Their breath begins to smell fruity.

The reason for this is not farfetched. Keto diet faithful's are known to have higher concentrations of ketones and one of these ketones is acetone, which characteristically smells fruity. Studies have it recorded that the acetone is mostly eliminated via the lungs and breath.

Some have an issue with their breath smelling fruity, but if you want to follow keto, this is something you may have to contend with until you stop. Bad smell lasts for few days.

4. Change in the frequency of periods

Well, only females should be bothered about this side effect, though this may not be the case for every female following keto diet. Most females, who practice keto diet experience an irregularity in the frequency of their periods.

In the event of ketosis, comes weight loss, which also results in hormonal imbalances: there may seem to be a decline in the concentration of follicle-stimulating hormone, estrogen, progesterone, luteinizing hormone, gonadotropin-releasing hormone.

All these hormones are associated with ovulation, if they are in low concentration, ovulation may not take place, and if ovulation doesn't take place, expecting menstruation would be considered as far-fetched– since it is the biological process that comes after ovulation. But as stated earlier, not all ladies who practice keto dieting may get to experience this.

5. Dehydration and elimination of electrolytes

While the idea of weight loss is exciting, it would be rash to pay no attention to its complication. As more weight is being lost, the body's water concentration is tampered with; because weight is largely associated with water.

Electrolytes are lost in the event of ketosis, insulin level drops and is largely responsible for maintaining the concentration of the body's electrolytes. These electrolytes include – sodium, potassium, calcium etc. – which are highly essential for proper body functioning of the body.

One way around this is to take in enough supplements – like potassium citrate – and water as you go about this diet plan; by doing so you can salvage the consequences that comes with indulging in keto diet.

CHAPTER 10

REMEDIES

As emphasized in the first paragraph, these side effects discussed are not to scare you away from keto diet, instead to inform better on what is at stake and develop ways around them. Keto diet already proves too beneficial to pass up on. However, these side effects should not be ignored, which has led me to offer possible strategies, which may have been already highlighted, on how to evade some of these consequences.

Here are a few of them:

1. Consult medical practitioners before going keto

If you already have a medical condition like diabetes or any kidney diseases, discretion is advised before following keto diet. Your doctor will advise you better on whether it is safe for you to follow keto diet or not. If you don't know whether you have a medical condition or not, it is advisable to do the necessary tests under the guidance of your doctor, before proceeding with the diet plan.

2. Take supplements

Since going keto may restrict you from eating certain fruits and vegetables because of their high caloric content, which are generally rich in vitamins and minerals, it is advised to take supplements like potassium, so as to not let your body miss out on essential nutrients that are beneficial.

3. Consult a dietician

The whole idea of following a diet plan is to observe what goes into your body; there is really no point going keto if you won't do it well. So, in essence, consult a dietician to map out a diet plan that you can stick to and also in any case you want to eat something you aren't sure if it's healthy or not.

4. Drink as much water as possible

One can't overemphasize the essence of drinking enough water. Keto primary line of focus is losing weight, when weight is lost, the body's water level is altered and dehydration is a likely consequence. To salvage the situation you have to drink as much water as you can.

While keto diet is highly beneficial, be conscious of the side effects that have been discussed in this chapter and take the necessary precautions – which have been discussed too in this chapter – to put you on top of whatever side effect that may pose a threat to continuing your diet plan.

1. Roasted Butternut Squash Soup

Ingredients

1 large butternut squash, peeled and diced (without pips)

2 potatoes, peeled and chopped

3 tablespoons of extra virgin olive oil

Pinch of salt

Black pepper

1 tablespoon butter

1 chopped onion

1 celery stalk

1 big carrot, chopped

1 tablespoon fresh thyme and more to garnish

1 quarter of low sodium chicken broth

How to make Roasted Butternut Squash Soup

1. Preheat the oven to 400°. On a large baking sheet, mix butternut squash and potatoes with 2 tablespoons of olive oil and season it with salt and pepper. Roast for 25 minutes.

2. Meanwhile, melt butter and the remaining tablespoon of olive oil in a large saucepan over medium heat. Add onions, celery, carrots and cook for 7 to 10 minutes until soft. Season with salt, pepper and thyme.

3. Add the roasted pumpkin and potatoes and pour over the chicken broth. Boil for 10 minutes and then mix the soup with a dip mixer to make it creamy. (Alternatively, you can carefully put the hot soup in a blender.)

Total servings 4

NUTRITION (1 serving)

CALORIES	198
PROTEINS	7 g
FATS	22g
CARBS	3g

2. Keto instant pot chicken soup

Ingredients

1 whole chicken with skin

5 chopped celery stalks

2 medium carrots, peeled and chopped

1 medium onion, peeled and chopped

3 garlic cloves, peeled and chopped

2 tablespoons (6 g) Italian spice

2 litres (8 cups) of water

2 tablespoons (30 g) salt

1 teaspoon (1 g) black pepper

1/4 cup parsley (4 g), chopped (garnish to serve)

How to make Keto instant pot chicken soup

1. Place every ingredient (except parsley) in the instant pot.

2. Put Instant Pot on manual high pressure for 25 minutes.

3. Release the pressure slowly and enjoy it.

Total servings 6

NUTRITION (1 serving)

CALORIES	212
PROTEINS	46 g
FATS	2 g
CARBS	2 g

3. Keto Chicken Enchilada Soup

Ingredients

2 teaspoons of olive oil (10 ml)

1 red onion (110 g), peeled and finely chopped

2 teaspoons of cumin powder (4 g)

1 teaspoon cayenne pepper (2 g)

2 garlic cloves (6 g), peeled and finely chopped

4 chicken breasts (800 g), skinless and without bones

2 teaspoons of dried oregano (2 g)

3 1/2 cups of chicken broth (840 ml)

3/4 can tomato cubes (300 g)

1 yellow pepper (120 g), chopped

Salt and pepper for seasoning

2 tomato slices (45 g), cut in half to garnish

1 large avocado (200 g), diced

Coriander, finely chopped for garnishing

1/2 red pepper (7 g)

How to make Keto Chicken Enchilada Soup

1. Cut red onions and reserve 2 tablespoons for garnishing.

2. Cook onions in a pan with olive oil until tender and caramelized.

3. Halfway through, add cumin, cayenne pepper and garlic.

4. Add onions, chicken and oregano to the slow cooker. Pour chicken broth and tomatoes. Cover and cook over high heat for 2.5 hours.

5. Add pepper and cook for another 30 minutes.

6. Season the chicken with salt and pepper (after shredding the chicken).

7. If desired, decorate with a small slice of tomato, avocado, cilantro, peppers and onions.

8. Serve hot.

Total servings 8

NUTRITION (1 serving)

CALORIES	212
PROTEINS	35 g
FATS	8g
CARBS	3g

4. Bacon Cauliflower Chowder

Ingredients

4 bacon slices

1 medium yellow onion, chopped

2 medium carrots, peeled and chopped

2 celery stalks, chopped

Salt to taste

Black pepper to taste

2 cloves of garlic chopped

2 tablespoons of flour

2 sprigs of thyme, striped and chopped

Cut 1 cauliflower into small florets

1 quarter vegetable broth

1 tablespoon whole milk

How to make Bacon Cauliflower Chowder

1. Cook the bacon until crispy in a large saucepan over medium heat.

2. Transfer to a plate covered with paper towel and drain all except two tablespoons of fat.

3. Add onions, carrots and celery in the pot.

4. Season with salt and pepper. Cook until tender, about 5 minutes.

5. Add garlic and cook until fragrant, 1 minute. Stir in flour and cook for another 2 minutes. Add thyme and cauliflower.

6. Add broth and milk and bring it to boil. Reduce the heat immediately and cook until the cauliflower is tender (about 15 minutes).

7. Season it with salt and pepper.

8. Garnish with bacon before serving.

Total servings 2

NUTRITION (1 serving)

CALORIES	250
PROTEINS	22 g
FATS	15g
CARBS	3g

5. Avocado Chipotle Soup

Ingredients

2 big avocados

3 cups / 710 ml chicken broth or vegetable stock

1 cup / 240 ml full fat sour cream

½ -1 teaspoon (or to taste) chipotle

Sea salt OR Himalayan salt to taste

How to make Avocado Chipotle Soup

1. Cut the avocados in half. Remove the pits and throw them away. Put the flesh in a blender.

2. Mix the avocados until smooth. If necessary, add a little broth to facilitate the mixing process.

3. In a large pot bring the remaining broth to a boil, and then remove from heat.

4. Add avocado puree, sour cream and chipotle. Mix well with a spoon until everything is smooth. In case of lumps, mix the soup until smooth with a submersible mixer or a normal blender.

5. Warm it up again until it is hot, but do not let it boil (this is very important if the mixture boils, it may separate).

6. If desired, season with salt.

7. Divide the soup into soup cups.

8. If desired, serve with lemon or lime wedges and chopped fresh herbs (such as parsley or coriander).

Total servings 4

NUTRITION (1 serving)

CALORIES	235
PROTEINS	12 g
FATS	26g
CARBS	4g

6. Homemade Thai chicken soup

Ingredients

1 whole chicken

1 stalk of lemon grass, cut into large pieces

20 fresh basil leaves (10 for the slow cooker and 10 for garnishing)

5 thick slices of fresh ginger

1 lime

1 tablespoon salt

Extra salt to taste

How to make Thai chicken soup

1. Add chicken, lemon grass, 10 basil leaves, ginger and salt to the slow cooker.

2. Fill the casserole with water.

3. Cook on low heat for 8-10 hours.

4. Ladle the broth in a bowl, season with salt, squeeze fresh lime juice and garnish with chopped basil leaves

Total servings 4

NUTRITION (1 serving)

CALORIES	260
PROTEINS	55 g
FATS	4 g
CARBS	2 g

7. Hamburger stew

Ingredients

2 tablespoons of olive oil

2 pounds of ground beef

1 small chopped onion

3 garlic cloves chopped

32 ounces/ 4 cups of beef broth

15 ounces / 1 ¾ cups of canned or fresh pumpkin puree

10 ounces/ 1 ¼ cups of chopped radish

4 sliced celery stalks

1 1/2 tablespoons of sea salt

1 teaspoon ground black pepper

1 teaspoon dried oregano

1 teaspoon dried basil

1 teaspoon parsley flakes

1/2 teaspoon marjoram

1/4 teaspoon sage

10 ounces / 1 ¼ cups of chopped spinach (fresh or frozen)

How to make hamburger stew

Stove:
1. Heat the oil in the Dutch oven over medium heat.

2. Add minced meat, onions and garlic. Cook until the meat is golden brown.

3. Add broth, pumpkin, radishes, celery and spices. Bring to a boil. Reduce the heat and simmer for 20 minutes.

4. Add the spinach and cook for another 10 minutes.

5. Adjust the spices as needed.

Crock Pot:

1. Fry the minced meat with onions and garlic and place in the slow cooker if necessary.

2. Add broth, pumpkin, radishes, celery and spices.

3. Cook on low heat for 2-3 hours. Spinach can be added in the last hour.

Total servings 8

NUTRITION (1 serving)

CALORIES	425
PROTEINS	32.5 g
FATS	26g
CARBS	3g

8. Broccoli cheese soup

Ingredients

4 cups of broccoli (florets)

4 garlic cloves (chopped)

3 1/2 cups of chicken broth (or vegetable stock or broth)

1 cup heavy cream

3 cups of cheddar cheese (pre-shredded)

How to make Broccoli cheese soup

1. Sauté garlic in a large saucepan over medium heat for 1 minute.

2. Add chicken broth, heavy cream and chopped broccoli.

3. Increase the heat to bring to a boil, after it starts boiling, reduce the heat and simmer for 10 to 20 minutes until the broccoli is tender.

4. Gradually add the grated cheddar cheese and stir until melted. (Add ½ cup (64 g)),

5. Simmer and stir until completely melted, then repeat with other ½ cup (64 g) until all the cheese is used up.

6. Make sure to keep it at very low heat and avoid hot temperature to avoid seizures.

Total servings 6

NUTRITION (1 serving)

CALORIES	216
PROTEINS	11 g
FATS	27g
CARBS	2g

9. Keto chicken ramen soup

Ingredients

1 sliced chicken breast

4 cups (960 ml) chicken broth (or chicken bouillon)

2 eggs

1 zucchini made into noodles

1 tablespoon ginger, chopped

2 garlic cloves, peeled and chopped

2 tablespoons (30 ml) of Tamari sauce

3 tablespoons (45 ml) of avocado oil to cook with

How to make Keto chicken ramen soup

1. Fry the chicken slices in the avocado oil in a large pan until cooked and browned.

2. Boil 2 eggs and cut them in half.

3. Pour chicken broth into a large saucepan and simmer with ginger, garlic, tamari sauce and add zucchini noodles for 2 to 3 minutes.

4. Divide the broth into 2 bowls, bring the eggs to a boil and slice the chicken breast.

5. Season with extra hot sauce or tamari sauce.

Total servings 6

NUTRITION (1 serving)

CALORIES	250
PROTEINS	20 g
FATS	26 g
CARBS	4 g

10. Tomato basil soup

Ingredients

1 tin (28 ounces)/ 800 grams of whole plum tomatoes

2 cups of filtered water

1.5 teaspoons coarse salt kosher

1/2 teaspoon onion powder

1/4 teaspoon garlic powder

1 tablespoon butter

8 ounces/ 1 cup of mascarpone cheese

2 tablespoons of granulated erythritol sweetener

1 teaspoon apple cider vinegar

1/4 teaspoon dried basil leaves

1/4 cup basil pesto

How to make tomato basil soup

1. Mix canned tomatoes, water, salt, onion powder and garlic powder in a medium saucepan.

2. Bring to a boil over medium heat, and then simmer for 2 minutes.

3. Remove from heat, place in a blender and blend properly.

4. Go back to the stove; add butter and mascarpone cheese to the soup.

5. Stir over low heat until melted and creamy - about 2 minutes

6. Remove from heat and stir in sweetener, cider vinegar, dried basil and pesto.

7. Serve hot.

8. Store leftovers in a sealed container in the refrigerator for up to 5 days or in the freezer for up to 3 months.

Total servings 3

Nutrition (per serving)

Calories: 280
Fat: 33g
Carbohydrates: 7g
Protein: 8g

11. Keto Paleo Cabbage Roll Soup

Ingredients

2 tablespoons of butter or ghee

2 tablespoons of olive oil

1 cup diced onion

4 cloves of garlic

1 1/2 pounds of ground beef

1/2 pound minced pork

6 cups of beef broth

3 teaspoons of dried oregano leaves

2 teaspoons of sea salt

2 teaspoons of smoked paprika

2 teaspoons of garlic powder

2 teaspoons of onion powder

1 teaspoon black pepper

1/2 teaspoon dried thyme

16 ounces / 2 cups of diced tomatoes, drained

8 ounces / 1 cup tomato paste

2 tablespoons of chopped fresh parsley

1 large cabbage, halved and sliced

3 cups of cauliflower

How to make cabbage roll soup

1. In a large pan, heat the butter and olive oil over medium heat.

2. Add onions and garlic. Cook until onions are translucent and garlic is fragrant.

3. Put the ground beef and pork in the pan. Cook until browned and drain off excess fat.

4. Add Beef broth, oregano, sea salt, paprika, garlic powder, onion powder, black pepper, thyme, tomatoes, tomato paste, parsley, cabbage add riced cauliflower.

5. Bring to a boil, reduce the heat and simmer for 30 to 45 minutes.

Total servings 8

NUTRITION (1 serving)

CALORIES	350
PROTEINS	26 g
FATS	34g
CARBS	6g

12. Chicken kale soup

Ingredients

1 tablespoon olive oil

2 pounds of boneless chicken breast

16 ounces/ 2 cups of chicken bone bouillon

1/3 cup onion

1/2 cup olive oil

32 ounces/ 4 cups of chicken broth

5 ounces/ 2/3 cup kale leaves

Salt to taste

How to cook chicken kale soup

1. Heat 1 tablespoon olive oil in a large pan over medium heat.

2. Season the chicken with salt and pepper and add to the pan.

3. Reduce the temperature to a medium level, cover the pan and let the chicken cook for about 15 minutes or until the internal temperature reaches 165 ° F.

4. Chop the chicken and place in the casserole.

5. Mix chicken broth, chopped onion, and olive oil until smooth. Pour into the casserole.

6. Add remaining ingredients to the casserole, and cover.

7. Cook over low heat for about 3 hours, stirring once or twice.

Total servings 8

NUTRITION (1 serving)

CALORIES	289
PROTEINS	26.5 g
FATS	27.5g
CARBS	4.5g

13. Greek Lemon Chicken Soup

Ingredients

10 cups of chicken broth

3 tablespoons of olive oil

8 cloves of garlic

1 sweet onion

1 large lemon, serrated

2 chicken breasts without bones and without skin

1 cup Israeli couscous

1/2 teaspoon ground red pepper

2 ounces/ 4 tablespoons of crumbled feta

1/3 cup chopped chive

How to make Greek lemon chicken soup

1. Place olive oil over medium heat in a large pot. Peel the onion. Then cut into four pieces and cut into thin strips.

2. Once the oil is hot, fry the onion and chopped garlic for 3 to 4 minutes.

3. Add the chicken broth, raw chicken breast, lemon zest and crushed red pepper to the casserole dish.

4. Increase heat, cover the pan and bring to a boil. After it boils reduce heat and simmer for 5 minutes.

5. Season with couscous, 1 teaspoon salt and black pepper. Simmer for 5 minutes. Then turn off the fire.

6. Remove both chicken breasts with pliers from the pot.

7. Use a fork and forceps to shred the chicken.

8. Then put it back in the pot. Stir in baked feta cheese and chives.

9. Taste, salt and pepper as needed. Serve hot.

Total servings 6

NUTRITION (1 serving)

CALORIES	266.7
PROTEINS	24 g
FATS	25g
CARBS	3g

14. Keto Soup with Sausage, Peppers, and Spinach

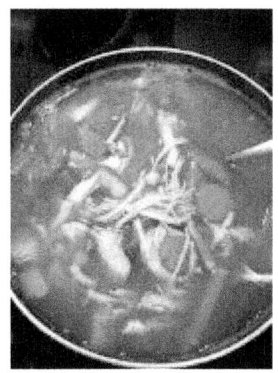

Ingredients

2 tablespoons of extra virgin olive oil

1 pound pork sausages

1 medium red pepper, diced

1/2 medium Poblano pepper, diced

3 celery stalks, diced

1 teaspoon dried basil

1 teaspoon dried oregano

1 teaspoon dried rosemary

1 1/2 teaspoons of chilli powder

1 teaspoon ground cumin

1/2 teaspoon ground cinnamon

Sea salt and black pepper to taste

6 cups of unsweetened organic chicken broth

2 cups of spinach

1 cup cheddar cheese Jack, grated

How to make Keto Soup with Sausages, Peppers, and Spinach

1. Heat olive oil in a Dutch oven or large saucepan over medium heat.

2. Add sausages. Cook for 5 minutes and stir occasionally until the sausages are no longer pink.

3. Break the sausage into small pieces with a wooden spoon.

4. Add paprika (red and poblano), celery, oregano, basil, rosemary, chili powder, cumin and cinnamon in the pot.

5. Season with salt and pepper. Stir occasionally until vegetables gets softened (5-6 minutes).

6. Add the chicken broth. Simmer for 20 minutes, stirring occasionally. Add the spinach and cook until the spinach wilts (about 4-5 minutes).

7. Remove from heat. Serve immediately with cheese and, if desired, diced Poblano peppers.

Total servings 6

NUTRITION (1 serving)

CALORIES	333.33
PROTEINS	22 g
FATS	32g
CARBS	5.7g

15. Pressure Electric Cooker pot chili

Ingredients

1.5 pounds of ground beef

1 tablespoon vegetable oil

2 tablespoons of salted butter

1 medium-sized yellow onion, finely diced

1-2 Poblano peppers, cut into small cubes and remove the seeds

1 small jalapeño pepper, cut into small cubes with the seeds removed

1 small Habanero pepper, cut in half with the seeds

8 oz / 1 cup tomato sauce

16 oz / 2 cups of tomato cubes

12 oz /1 and ½ cups of rotel

1 tablespoon hoisin sauce

1/4 cup taco sauce

1 tablespoon worcester sauce

1/2 teaspoon kosher salt

1 teaspoon Italian spice mixture

1 teaspoon dried coriander

2 tablespoons of cumin

1/2 tablespoon chili powder

1 teaspoon spiced salt

1 teaspoon celery salt

1 teaspoon Creole spice blend

4 tablespoons of chili base

How to make Pressure Electric Cooker POT CHILI

1. Heat butter and vegetable oil in the saucepan.

2. Once the butter has melted and the oil is sizzling, add onions, poblano, jalapeno and habanero peppers and stir for 5 minutes until tender.

3. Add garlic and cook for another minute.

4. Remove the habanero pepper only once and discard it

5. Then add the minced meat and stir until it is cooked and crumbled and gets a little brown (about 3 minutes).

6. Add beer, diced tomatoes, rotel, tomato sauce, taco sauce and Hoisin sauce. Stir the bottom of the pot and peel it off

7. Now add kosher salt, Italian seasoning, cumin, chili powder, dried coriander, spiced salt, celery salt and Tony's Creole spice

8. Stir again until well combined

9. Add the drained and rinsed red kidney beans, but do NOT mix them with the rest. Simply smooth them by placing them on top of the chili

10. Attach the lid and cook on high heat

11. When done, allow it to cool.

12. Mix well, add Chili, than Bouillon and stir again.

13. Pour into small bowls and garnish with grated cheese, sour cream or fried beans.

Total servings 8

NUTRITION (1 serving)

CALORIES	260
PROTEINS	23 g
FATS	25g
CARBS	3.7g

16. Pressure Electric Cooker pot vegetarian chili

Ingredients

1 tablespoon olive oil

2 garlic cloves crushed

1 small white onion chopped

1 big Poblano chili

1 jalapeño diced and without the seeds

1 tablespoon chili powder

2 tablespoons of caraway tea

1 teaspoon paprika

1 teaspoon sea salt

1/4 teaspoon cayenne pepper

16 oz / 2 cups of tomato cubes with pepper

1 sweet potato, peeled and cut into small pieces

How to cook vegetarian chili

1. Preheat the sauce pan.

2. Add olive oil and cover the pan.

3. Add onions, garlic and two peppers.

4. Stir and cook for 3 minutes or until the vegetables soften.

5. Mix all the spices.

6. Add all the beans, tomatoes with juice, sweet potatoes, water and corn.

7. Cook for 4 minutes on high heat.

8. If necessary, season with more salt and serve immediately with the desired toppings.

Total servings 4

NUTRITION (1 serving)

CALORIES	198
PROTEINS	9 g
FATS	19 g
CARBS	7 g

17. Beef stew

Ingredients

1 1/2 pounds of meat stew

1 tablespoon olive oil

1 teaspoon salt

1 teaspoon pepper

1 teaspoon Italian seasoning

2 tablespoons of Worcester sauce

3 garlic cloves chopped

1 large chopped onion

1 bag of 16 ounces/ 2 cups of carrot, sliced

Beef broth 2 1/2 cups

1 can / 1 and ½ cups of tomatoes

2 tablespoons of cornstarch

2 tablespoons of water

How to make Beef stew

1. Heat olive oil in a pan.

2. When the oil begins to sizzle, Add the meat and season with salt, pepper and Italian dressing.

3. Cook the meat until golden brown on all sides.

4. Add Worcestershire sauce, garlic, onions, carrots, potatoes and tomato sauce.

5. Boil at high pressure for 25 minutes.

6. Mix the cornstarch and cold water in a small bowl and stir in the stew until thick.

Total servings 8

NUTRITION (1 serving)

CALORIES	302
PROTEINS	32 g
FATS	20g
CARBS	5.2g

18. Italian meatball soup

Ingredients

2 tablespoons of extra virgin olive oil

1 large onion diced

8 chopped garlic cloves

2 large carrots, diced

1 cup chopped celery

3 tablespoons of tomato paste

1 cup marinara sauce

1 can mince tomatoes

20-25 fully cooked and frozen mini meatballs

1 teaspoon dried basil

1 teaspoon dried oregano

1/2 teaspoon red pepper flakes

1/2 teaspoon black pepper

1/2 teaspoon salt if necessary

32 ounces / 4 cups of beef or vegetable broth I used beef broth

Garnish:

2 tablespoons of fresh parsley, diced

2 tablespoons of green onions, diced

1/4 cup of Parmesan or mozzarella

How to cook Italian meatball soup

1. Preheat your pan.

2. Add oil to the pan, add the chopped onions and the chopped garlic and fry for 2 to 3 minutes, stirring several times.

4. Add the carrots and cook for 1 minute.

5. Add the tomato paste and cook for another minute.

6. Add the remaining ingredients. Stir.

7. Cook for 5 minutes.

8. Serve with green onions, parsley and mozzarella.

Total servings 8

NUTRITION (1 serving)

CALORIES	206.5
PROTEINS	18 g
FATS	17g
CARBS	4.7g

19. Low carb chili

Ingredients

2 1/2 pounds of ground beef

1/2 large onion chopped

8 chopped garlic cloves

2, 16 oz / 2 cups of tomatoes

1 oz / 2 tablespoons of tomato paste

2 tablespoons of Worcester sauce

1/4 cup chili powder

2 tablespoons of cumin soup

1 tablespoon dried oregano

2 teaspoons of sea salt

1 teaspoon black pepper

How to cook low carb chili

1. Preheat your pan.

2. Add chopped onion and cook for 5 to 7 minutes.

3. Add garlic and cook for a minute or less.

4. Add minced meat.

5. Cook for 8 to 10 minutes, separate with a spatula until golden brown.

6. Add the remaining ingredients to the pan and stir until all ingredients are well mixed.

8. It is also recommended to add a cup of water or broth.

9. Close the lid.

10. Cook for 30 minutes.

Total servings 8

NUTRITION (1 serving)

CALORIES	325
PROTEINS	30 g
FATS	15g
CARBS	5.7g

20. Spanish / Mexican soup

Ingredients

1 tablespoon olive oil

1 small onion chopped

2 garlic cloves chopped

½ red pepper, diced

½ yellow pepper, diced

½ green pepper, diced

1 small box of tomato paste

½ teaspoon chili powder

¼ teaspoon Ground cumin

1½ cups of cauliflower rice

1 tomato, no seeds and diced

How to cook spinach/ Mexican soup

1. Heat olive oil in a pan.

2. Add onions, garlic, red, yellow and green peppers and fry vegetables for 3 to 5 minutes.

3. Add broth, tomato paste, chili powder, ground cumin and mix well.

4. Then add the rinsed rice and stir again.

5. Garnish the rice with diced tomatoes.

6. Cook for 15 minutes.

7. Serve the rice with a side of vegetarian aioli and some parsley.

Total servings 2

NUTRITION (1 serving)

CALORIES	188
PROTEINS	12 g
FATS	18 g
CARBS	5.7g

21. Spinach soup

Ingredients

3 eggs

Salt

Pepper

Pinch nutmeg

2 cups of chicken broth

½ cup heavy cream

½ cup mozzarella cheese

300 grams of spinach

1 garlic (minced)

½ onion (chopped)

2 tablespoons of oil

How to make spinach soup

1. Heat oil in a pan, add onion and garlic.

2. Add spinach and cook until bright green (3 minutes approx)

3. Transfer to a blender and add 1 cup broth.

4. Blend properly

5. Transfer the mixture in a pan or skillet and add broth.

6. Bring to simmer and add cream and mozzarella.

7. Cook till the cheese melts.

8. Serve with hardboiled eggs.

Total servings 4

NUTRITION (1 serving)

CALORIES	175
PROTEINS	12 g
FATS	15 g
CARBS	4 g

22 Cheesy cream of cauliflower soup

Ingredients

1 cup parmesan

2 cups of mozzarella

2 cups of heavy cream

6 cups of chicken broth

2 heads of cauliflower

6 garlics (minced)

2 onions chopped

8 tablespoons of butter

How to make cheesy cream of cauliflower soup

1. Heat butter in a skillet, add onions and fry until golden brown.

2. Add cauliflower and garlic and cook for 4-6 minutes, then add broth and simmer until tender.

3. Transfer in a food processor and blend until smooth.

4. Then transfer to a skillet again and add cream and bring to simmer again. Stir in cheeses and serve.

Total servings 8

NUTRITION (1 serving)

CALORIES	340
PROTEINS	7 g
FATS	39 g
CARBS	2 g

23. Creamy leek and salmon soup

Ingredients

2 tablespoons of avocado oil

4 leeks, washed and cut

3 garlic cloves chopped

6 cups of seafood or chicken broth

2 tablespoon dried thyme leaves

1 pound of salmon in small pieces

1 ¾ cup of coconut milk

Salt and pepper to taste

How to make creamy leek and salmon soup

1. Heat the avocado oil in a large saucepan or oven over medium heat.

2. Add the chopped leek and the garlic and cook gently.

3. Pour the broth and add the thyme. Simmer for about 15 minutes and season with salt and pepper.

4. Add salmon and coconut milk to the pan. Simmer gently and simmer until the fish is opaque and tender.

5. Serve immediately!

Total servings 2

NUTRITION (1 serving)

CALORIES	255
PROTEINS	40 g
FATS	27g
CARBS	5 g

24. Creamy Garlic Chicken Soup

Ingredients

2 tablespoons of butter

2 cups of chopped chicken (1 big chicken breast)

4 ounces / ½ cup cream cheese cubes

2 tablespoons of Gusto Garlic spice Stacey Hawkins

16 ounces / 2 cups of chicken broth

1/4 cup thick cream

Salt to taste

How to make Creamy Garlic Chicken Soup

1. Melt the butter in a saucepan over medium heat.

2. Put the chopped chicken in the pan and coat with melted butter.

3. When the chicken gets warm, add cream cheese cubes and Stacey Hawkins Garlic Gusto. Mix to blend the ingredients.

4. Once the cream cheese is melted and evenly distributed, add chicken broth and cream. Bring to a boil, then reduce the heat and simmer for 3-4 minutes.

5. Season with salt and serve.

Total servings 6

NUTRITION (1 serving)

CALORIES	189
PROTEINS	11 g
FATS	19 g
CARBS	4.3 g

25. Ham and Green Bean Soup

Ingredients

1 quart / 4 cups of ham broth

1 quart / 4 cups of chicken broth

2 cups of water

2 tablespoons of bacon drippings

2 garlic cloves (chopped)

3 ounces / 6 tablespoons of onion (chopped)

Cut 1 pound of green beans into 1-inch pieces

1 pound of ham (in cubes)

1/2 teaspoon garlic powder

1 teaspoon salt

1/2 teaspoon aroma of liquid smoke

Salt and pepper

How to make ham and green beans soup

1. Chop the onions and garlic.

2. Put the bacon juice or oil in a large saucepan and heat over medium.

3. Fry the onions and garlic in oil until translucent.

4. If you do not use the remaining green beans, cut them off as well.

5. Pour the chicken and ham broth into the pan with water and bring to a boil.

6. Pour all the foam that forms at the top of the soup.

7. Add the green beans and cook for a few minutes.

8. Then add salt, smoke flavorings and garlic powder.

9. Simmer gently until the potatoes are cooked.

10. Add ham.

11. Adjust the spices and serve them.

Total servings 4

NUTRITION (1 serving)

CALORIES	220
PROTEINS	20 g
FATS	18 g
CARBS	5 g

26. Coconut soup with shrimp or chicken

Ingredients

Broth

4 cups of chicken broth

1.5 cups of fat coconut milk

1 organic lime

1 teaspoon dried lemongrass

1 cup fresh coriander

3 or 4 dried thai peppers or 1 sliced jalapeno

1 inch fresh galangal root or 1 inch fresh ginger root or 2 to 3 dried galangal roots

1 teaspoon sea salt

Soup

100 g raw wild caught shrimp or 100 g raw chicken meat

1 tablespoon coconut oil

30 g mushrooms sliced.

30 g red onion, chopped

1 tablespoon fish sauce or 1 finely chopped anchovy

Juice of 1 lime

1 tablespoon chopped cilantro for garnish

How to make Coconut soup with shrimp or chicken

Broth
1. Put all the ingredients in a saucepan and simmer for 20 minutes.

2. Strain through a fine mesh colander and pour back into the pan.

Soup
Boil the broth, than add shrimp or chicken, fish or anchovies.

Add the chopped onions and mushrooms.

Boil for about 10 minutes until the meat is cooked.

Add lime juice and serve in bowls of chopped cilantro as garnish.

Total servings 2

NUTRITION (1 serving)

CALORIES	390
PROTEINS	37 g
FATS	28g
CARBS	4.66g

27. Spicy Cauliflower Soup

Ingredients

1 large cauliflower (800 g)

1 or more small cauliflower (200 g)

1 small white onion (70 g)

2 cups of chicken broth, vegetable broth or bouillon, preferably homemade (480 ml / 16 oz / 2 cups)

1 sausage or medium spicy chorizo pepper (150 g)

3 tablespoons of ghee, lard or butter (45 g)

1/2 teaspoon salt

1 spring onion or chive for garnishing (15 g)

How to cook Spicy Cauliflower Soup

1. Wash the cauliflower and cut it into small bunches.

2. Grease a large Dutch saucepan with 2 tablespoons ghee and add finely chopped onions. Cook over medium heat until lightly browned. Add the cauliflower and cook for about 5 minutes by stirring. Add the chicken broth and cover with a lid. Cook for 10 minutes and remove from heat.

NOTE- I have used a Dutch stove, which is a heavy cast iron pot. It cooks your meat evenly and is ideal for meat and vegetable stews. I love preparing curries and soups

3. Cut the sausage into cubes. Peel the turnip and cut into small cubes or use more cauliflower - the stems are ideal for browning. Place on a thick frying pan greased with the remaining ghee and cook over medium heat until the sausages are crispy and the turnip is soft for about 8-10 minutes.

4. Add half of the chorizo-beet mixture to the soup. Smooth it with a blender. Season with salt and pepper. You can also add 1 cup thick whipped cream or grated cheddar cheese.

5. Put in a serving bowl, sprinkle with chorizo and turnips and drizzle with a little spicy oil. Garnish with spring onions or freshly cut chives and enjoy.

Total servings 4

NUTRITION (1 serving)

CALORIES	225
PROTEINS	15 g
FATS	20g
CARBS	4.86g

28. Sopa De Lima

Ingredients
2 chicken breasts

1/4 teaspoon chilli powder

1/4 teaspoon garlic powder

4 cups of organic chicken broth or homemade chicken broth

2 Serrano Chilli Pepper (Cut off all the seeds, scrape them and cut small pieces)

4 garlic cloves (peeled and chopped.)

2 chopped tomatoes

1 tablespoon of olive oil

1/3 lime juice

1/2 teaspoon lime zest

2 tablespoons of chopped fresh coriander

1 avocado peeled and chopped.

Dash sea salt

How to make sopa de lima

1. Preheat the oven to 400 ° C, insert a baking pan and grease it properly.

2. Put the chicken in the pan and sprinkle with chilli powder and garlic.

3. Cook the chicken for 20 minutes.

4. While the chicken is cooking, place a large pot on the stove.

5. Add the olive oil to the Dutch oven and fry the chopped garlic, the serrano peppers and the chopped onion for 3 minutes or until the vegetables soften.

6. Put the chopped tomatoes in the pot and simmer for another 2 minutes.

7. Add chicken broth and lime juice to the pan and mix, heat over low heat.

8. Remove the chicken from the oven and let it cool enough to cut it into small pieces.

9. Put the chopped chicken in the pot and stir.

10. Bring it to a boil, reduce the heat to a minimum and cover the lid.

11. Simmer for 20 minutes.

12. Add avocado pieces into each bowl.

13. Pour the soup over the avocado in bowls.

14. Garnish with coriander.

15. Can add sea salt to taste.

Total servings 6

NUTRITION (1 serving)

CALORIES	174
PROTEINS	16 g
FATS	12g
CARBS	4.86g

29. Easy Green Chicken Enchilada Soup

Ingredients

1/2 cup Salsa Verde

4 ounces/ ½ cup cream cheese

1 cup cheddar cheese, grated

2 cups of bouillon or chicken broth

2 cups of cooked chicken, grated

How to cook Easy Green Chicken Enchilada Soup

1. Mix salsa, cream cheese, cheddar cheese and chicken broth in a blender and stir until smooth. (You can also use an immersion mixer right in your pan for this step.)

2. Pour into a medium saucepan and simmer over medium heat do not bring to a boil).

3. Add the minced chicken and cook for another 3 to 5 minutes until everything is hot.

4. Garnish with grated cheddar and chopped cilantro.

Total servings 6

NUTRITION (1 serving)

CALORIES	174
PROTEINS	16 g
FATS	14g
CARBS	3

30. Chile Relleno chicken soup

Ingredients

5 Poblano peppers

2 tablespoons of butter

1/4 cup chopped onion

2 cloves of garlic chopped

1 teaspoon ground cumin

4 cups of chicken broth

Salt and pepper

1 lb boneless chicken breast, cut into 1/2-inch pieces

8 ounces/ 1 cup cream cheese, cut into cubes

3 1/2 cups of grated cheddar cheese

How to cook Chile Relleno chicken soup

1. Roast the Poblano peppers until the skin is charred and blistered. You can do this by having an open flame on a gas stove, or by heating your grill over high heat and placing Poblanos a few inches from the grill (turn it all the way around).

2. Place Poblanos in a bowl and cover with plastic wrap. Cool and rub the skin to remove as much as possible. Cut the seeds and place them in a food processor or blender to finely chop them.

3. Melt the butter in a large saucepan over medium heat. Add the onions and cook with frequent stirring until the mixture is translucent, about 5 minutes. Add the garlic, cumin and Poblanos and mix it for about 1 minute.

4. Stir in chicken broth and season with salt and pepper. Bring to a boil, reduce heat and simmer. Add chicken pieces and cook until chicken is cooked (about 10 minutes).

5. Add cream cheese and two cups of cheddar and stir until smooth.

6. Divide into 6 bowls to serve and sprinkle with 1/4 cup grated cheddar cheese.

Total serving 4

NUTRITION (1 serving)

CALORIES	575
PROTEINS	39.77g
FATS	37.99 g
CARBS	4.24 g

31. Keto-Bacon Cheeseburger Soup

Ingredients

4 cups of beef broth

1 medium-sized tomato (or a diced tomato of 14.5 ounces)

1/3 cup chopped dill pickles

2 tablespoons of Dijon mustard

2 tablespoons of Worcestershire sauce

2 tablespoons of chopped fresh parsley

1 teaspoon sea salt, more to taste

½ teaspoon black pepper

1 ½ pounds of ground beef

1 small diced onion

4 cloves of garlic

1 1/2 cups of grated cheddar cheese

1 cup heavy cream

8 slices of bacon crispy cooked and crumbled

Manual

Slow cooking instructions:

1. Heat the cooker over low heat.

2. Add beef broth, tomatoes, cucumbers, Dijon sauce, Worcestershire, parsley, sea salt and black pepper in the slow cooker.

3. In a large pan, cook ground beef, onions and garlic until ground beef is browned, over medium heat.

4. Drain off the excess fat and place in the slow cooker.

5. Cover and cook for 6 hours.

6. Stir in cheddar cheese and cream and cook for another hour.

7. Add the bacon just before serving.

Saucepan cooking Instructions:
1. Heat saucepan over medium heat.

2. Add the ground beef, onions, garlic and cook until the ground beef is golden yellow and cooked.

3. Add beef broth, tomatoes, cucumbers, Dijon sauce, Worcestershire, parsley, sea salt and black pepper. Bring to a boil, and then reduce the heat to low and simmer for 30 minutes.

4. Stir in cheddar cheese and cream, reduce heat, occasionally cover and stir, simmer for 30 minutes.

5. Add the bacon just before serving.

Total servings 8

NUTRITION (1 serving)

CALORIES	306
PROTEINS	35 g
FATS	22g
CARBS	4.44g

32. Pork and Tomato Soup

Ingredients

2 pounds of pork chops without bones, cut into 1 inch piece

1 tablespoon olive oil

1 tablespoon chopped garlic

1/2 cup chopped onion

1/2 cup dry white wine

1 cup chicken broth

2 cups of fresh tomatoes, chopped

1 cup water

2 tablespoons of fresh oregano, chopped

2 cups of finely chopped cauliflower "rice"

Salt and pepper

How to cook pork and tomato soup

1. Heat the olive oil in a heavy saucepan. Season the pork (or other meat) generously with salt and pepper.

2. Cook the meat on all sides for few minutes.

3. Add garlic and onions and cook for 2 minutes.

4. Add white wine, chicken broth, fresh tomatoes, water and bring to a boil.

5. Pour into a slow cooker and cook for 4 hours or until the meat is tender and peels off.

6. Add cauliflower and fresh oregano in the last 15-20 minutes. Serve hot.

Total servings 8

NUTRITION (1 serving)

CALORIES	294
PROTEINS	32 g
FATS	22g
CARBS	3

34. Instant chicken fajita soup

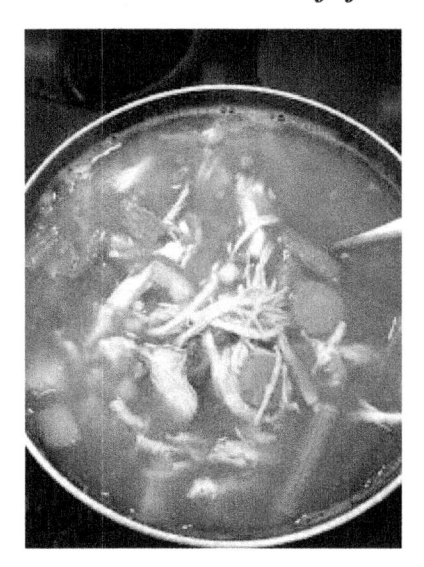

Ingredients

2 ½ lb chicken thighs

2 litres of chicken broth

10 oz /283 grams roasted tomatoes and green peppers

14.5 oz / 411 grams Diced tomatoes

10 ounces/ 283 grams of frozen small spices,

1 teaspoon salt

1 teaspoon black pepper

1teaspoon garlic powder

1 teaspoon chilli powder

How to make Instant chicken fajita soup

Instructions of pressure cooker:

1. Put all ingredients in a pressure cooker. Close and cook over high heat for 25 minutes (I used the soup setting of my instant pot).

2. Let the pressure relax in a natural way before opening the pressure cooker.

3. Remove the legs and chicken pieces and put them back in the pan.

4. Serve with lime chips, sour cream, grated cheese, chopped cilantro and avocado.

Notes on the Slow Cooker:
As above in your pressure cooker, but cook on high heat for 4 to 6 hours.

Total servings 6

NUTRITION (1 serving)

CALORIES	283
PROTEINS	35 g
FATS	21g
CARBS	6

35. Turkey soup, kale and pumpkin

Ingredients

1 pound sweet Italian turkey sausage

1/2 cup chopped onion

3 cups of chopped squash or butternut squash

4 cups of chopped kale

4 cups of chicken broth

4 cups of water

How to cook turkey soup

1. Cook the sausages in a medium saucepan. Add the onions and fry until translucent. Pour broth and water into the pan and bring to a boil than reduce heat.

2. Add cabbage and squash and cook until the squash is soft, about 20 minutes.

3. Serve hot, garnish with grated Parmesan cheese and crushed red pepper cakes.

Total servings 6

NUTRITION (1 serving)

CALORIES	186
PROTEINS	21.6g
FATS	12g
CARBS	4

36. Thai Tom Saap Pork Chop Soup

Ingredients

1 pound pork ribs (if possible cut into small 2-inch pieces) (you can also use other meat if you want)

Cut 2 red shallots into large pieces (or use 1 large yellow onion)

3-4 small stems of lemon grass, chopped

10 thick slices of galangal (or ginger)

8 cups of water

10 kaffir lime leaves

2 tablespoons of fish sauce

Salt to taste

Optional: peppers, spring onions for garnish

How to cook Thai Tom Saap Pork Chop Soup

1. Put the pork ribs in a large pot of water and cook for 10 minutes, and then pour away the liquid with the foam.

2. Pour about 8 cups of fresh water into the pan with the ribs and add shallot, lemongrass, galangal and salt to the pan.

3. Simmer on low heat for 1 hour with the lid.

4. Make sure the ribs are tender, and then add the kaffir lime leaves (chilli if you like spicy and if you have no AIP), the fish sauce, the juice of 1 lime and salt to your taste.

Total servings 4

NUTRITION (1 serving)

CALORIES	262
PROTEINS	29 g
FATS	16 g
CARBS	5

37. Creamy Soup with Cauliflower and Keto Ham

Ingredients

6 cups of cauliflower florets

6 cups of chicken broth

2 cups of water

1/2 teaspoon garlic powder

1/2 teaspoon onion powder

3 cups of chopped ham

2 tablespoons of apple cider vinegar

1 tablespoon fresh thyme leaves

2 tablespoons of Butter (or ghee, bacon fat or coconut oil)

Salt and ground black pepper to taste

How to cook Creamy Soup with Cauliflower and Keto Ham

1. Mix cauliflower, broth, water, garlic powder and onion powder in a large saucepan.

2. Bring to a boil and simmer for 20-30 minutes, until the cauliflower is soft.

3. Place in a large blender and mix until the mixture is smooth.

4. Stir in the ham and thyme leaves and cook for another 10 minutes.

5. Add butter and apple cider vinegar. Remove from heat and season with salt and pepper.

6. Serve hot.

NUTRITION (per cup)

CALORIES	125
PROTEINS	13 g
FATS	7 g
CARBS	5 g

38. Bacon Stew

Ingredients

½ pound unsalted organic bacon in strips

2 pounds of grass-fed and finished chuck roast, cut into small pieces

2 large organic red onions, peeled and sliced

1 garlic clove, peeled and crushed

1 small kale or Savoy

Celtic sea salt

Fresh black pepper to taste

1 sprig of fresh organic thyme

1 cup of homemade beef broth

How to cook Bacon stew

1. Add in the following order to your slow cooker:

Slices of bacon at the bottom

Onion slices and garlic

Chuck roast

Thyme

Broth

2. Add few pinches of sea salt and a good amount of fresh black pepper.

3. Cook on low heat for 7 hours.

4. Serve in bowls.

Total servings 8

NUTRITION (1 serving)

CALORIES	428
PROTEINS	48 g
FATS	20g
CARBS	9 g

39. Asian Noodle Soup

Ingredients

For meatballs:

1 pound ground pork (or turkey)

1 egg

1/3 cup almond flour

1 teaspoon chopped ginger

1/3 cup chopped spring onions

1 tablespoon gluten-free soy sauce

1/2 teaspoon garlic powder

1/2 teaspoon salt

For the broth:

1 teaspoon sesame oil

2 teaspoons of chopped ginger

1 teaspoon chopped garlic

32 oz (4 cup) chicken broth

2 cups of water

1 tablespoon gluten-free soy sauce

1 tablespoon fish sauce

1/2 teaspoon red pepper flakes

1/2teaspoon salt

Put soup together:

3 cups of keto friendly noodles drained and rinsed,

2 cups of grated Napa cabbage

1/4 cup radish sticks

1/4 cup grated carrots

1/2 cup chopped spring onions

1/2 cup chopped cilantro

6 lime wedges

How to cook Asian Noodle Soup

For meatballs:

1. Mix all meatballs ingredients in a medium bowl and mix well.

2. Form 24 meatballs and place on a baking tray.

3. Bake at 375 degrees (F) for 12 minutes or until cooked.

For the Broth:

1. Heat sesame oil in a medium saucepan and add chopped garlic and ginger.

2. Bake for about 1 minute.

3. Add chicken stock, water, soy sauce, fish sauce, red pepper flakes and salt.

4. Bring to a boil and simmer for at least 10 minutes.

5. Filter the broth to remove the solids and place in the pan.

6. Try and adapt the spices to your wishes.

7. Bring to a boil shortly before serving.

Put soup together:

1. Put about 1/2 cup of shiratake noodles in a soup bowl.

2. Garnish with four meatballs, a handful of cabbage and a dash of radish, carrots, spring onions and cilantro.

3. Pour about 1 cup of hot broth into the bowl.

4. Wait about 2 minutes for the ingredients to warm, squeeze a lime wedge and serve.

Approximate nutrition information:

4 meatballs: 203 calories, 15 g fat, 1 g carbohydrates, 16 g protein

1 cup brew: 23 calories, 1 g fat, 1.5 g carbohydrates, 1 g protein

Pasta and vegetables as indicated above: 15 calories, 0 g fat, 2 g net carbohydrates, 0 g protein

The recipe is the sum: 241 calories, 16 grams of fat, 4.5 grams of net carbohydrates, 17 grams of protein

Total servings 8

NUTRITION (1 serving)

CALORIES	240
PROTEINS	17 g
FATS	16 g
CARBS	4.5 g

40. Turkey and Butternut Soup with Ginger and Turmeric

Ingredients

1 cup turkey carcass

2 or 3 turkey necks

1 tablespoon apple cider vinegar

2 or 3 celery

1 organic carrot

1 tablespoon whole peppercorns

1 tablespoon of Celtic sea salt

2 inch fresh ginger root (OR ½ teaspoon ginger powder)

2 inch fresh turmeric root (or ½ teaspoon ginger powder)

For the soup

1 cup organic butternut squash, peeled and diced

4 ounces of turkey meat, saved from the neck of the turkey

Manual

1. First make the broth:

2. Dip turkey pieces and vegetables in about 1 litre of water in a large pot.

3. Add apple cider vinegar and sea salt.

4. Bring the water to a boil and cook it over low heat for about 8 hours. You can leave the pot uncovered or partially uncovered to concentrate the broth.

5. After about 4 hours of cooking, carefully remove the brewing neck and remove all meat. Then put the bones back in the pot.

6. Put the meat aside - can be refrigerated for up to a week.

To pour the broth:

1. Drain the bone stock with a fine mesh sieve and discard the bones.

2. Put the broth in a clean, cool pan.

3. Rub or chop the ginger and turmeric roots after thoroughly washing them. (If you use powder, put it with the broth in the pot).

4. Add the grated roots to the broth and simmer for about 1 hour.

5. After one hour, filter the mixture again through the fine sieve and discard the solid parts.

For the soup:

1. Put the broth back in the pan.

2. At this stage, there should be about 2 litres of broth, which can vary slightly depending on the heat intensity at which you simmer the broth. The measure is only a general guideline!

3. Add the butternut squash.

4. Simmer for about 30 minutes or until the pumpkin is tender.

5. Add the turkey meat to the soup and simmer for another 10 minutes.

6. Serve hot!

Total servings 8

NUTRITION (1 serving)

CALORIES	108
PROTEINS	6 g
FATS	7.5g
CARBS	3.25 g

41. Chilli with White Turkey and Light

Ingredients

1 pound organic turkey (or ground beef, lamb or pork)

2 cups of cauliflower

2 tablespoons of coconut oil

1/2 onion

2 cloves of garlic

2 cups of coconut milk (or heavy cream)

1 tablespoon mustard

1 teaspoon salt, black pepper, thyme, celery salt, garlic powder

How to cook Chili with White Turkey and Light

1. Heat the coconut oil in a large pot.

2. Chop the onion and garlic. Add it to the hot oil. Stir for 2-3 minutes.

3. Add the chopped turkey.

4. Break with the spatula and stir constantly until it crumbles. Add spice mixture and cauliflower and mix well.

5. Once the meat is golden yellow, add the coconut milk, simmer for 5-8 minutes, stirring often.

6. At this point it is ready to be served.

Suggestions for filling:

Avocados

Jalapenos

Bacon

Grated aged cheddar cheese

Cherry tomatoes

Spicy sauce

Total servings 7

NUTRITION (1 serving)

CALORIES	388
PROTEINS	28.8 g
FATS	30.5 g
CARBS	5.5 g

42. Thai Beef and Broccoli Soup

Ingredients

2 tablespoons of avocado oil or fat of your choice

1 onion, chopped

2 tablespoons of Thai green curry paste, adjust to taste

2-inch knob ginger, minced

2 garlic cloves, minced

1 Serrano pepper, minced

1 pound ground beef

3 tablespoons of coconut

2 teaspoons of fish sauce

½ teaspoon salt

½ teaspoon black pepper

4 cups of beef bone broth or chicken stock

2 large broccolis cut into florets

1 cup full-fat canned coconut milk

Cilantro for garnishing

Manual

1. Add the oil and onions to a dutch oven or pan and cook for 10 minutes, or until the onions begins to turn golden.

2. Add the curry paste, ginger, garlic and Serrano pepper and stir for 1 minute.

3. Add the ground beef, coconut, fish sauce, salt and pepper and cook until the beef is nearly brown.

4. Add broth; reduce the heat to low-medium. Cover the pot with a lid and cook for 20 minutes.

5. Add the broccoli florets and coconut milk to the pot, cover and cook for another 10 minutes.

6. Remove the lid, increase heat to high and simmer for 5 minutes.

7. Garnish with cilantro.

Total servings 5

NUTRITION (1 serving)

CALORIES	278
PROTEINS	25 g
FATS	21 g
CARBS	7.3 g

43. Good Ole South Soup

Ingredients

3 tablespoons of ghee or organic butter

1 large onion (chopped)

1 pound fully cooked, uncut ham steak cooked in cubes

2-3 cloves of garlic

2 celery stalks, chopped

2 carrots, peeled and chopped

6 cups of chicken broth or vegetables broth

4 cups of chopped kale (well rinsed and middle vein and discarded stems)

6 cups of chopped collards (well rinsed, as well as medium vein and discarded stems)

Mustard or turnip

1 tablespoon apple cider vinegar

1 tablespoon Sriracha (or hot favorite sauce)

Sea salt and ground pepper to taste

Manual

1. Heat the butter, onions, ham, garlic, celery and carrots in a Dutch oven or in a heavy saucepan. Cook over medium heat and stir until the onions are translucent.

2. Add broth and scrape the pieces off the bottom of the pot. Add vegetables, apple cider vinegar, Sriracha, salt & pepper.

3. Bring to a boil. Reduce the heat and cover it.

4. Simmer for 1.5 hours. If necessary, taste and add more salt and / or pepper.

5. Be happy!

Total servings 6

NUTRITION (1 serving)

CALORIES	282
PROTEINS	26 g
FATS	22 g
CARBS	6.3 g

44. Chile with low Carbohydrate Beans

Ingredients

2 tablespoons of butter (or ghee)

2 chopped peppers

1 yellow onion, chopped

1 cup chopped celery

1 pound ground beef

1 pound Italian bratwurst

28 ounces / 3 and ½ cups of diced tomatoes

16 ounces/2 cups of tomato sauce

2 cups of beef broth

8 ounces /1 cup heavily brewed coffee

1 tablespoon caraway

2 tablespoons of chilli powder (add more to make it spicy)

1 teaspoon garlic powder

1 teaspoon onion powder

1 tablespoon oregano powder

1 teaspoon salt

1 teaspoon black pepper

How to cook Chile with low Carbohydrate Beans

1. In a large pan melt butter over medium heat.

2. Add the chopped peppers, onion and celery and fry for 5-7 minutes until tender. Put the vegetables in the pan and set it aside.

3. Add ground beef and ground Italian sausages. Cook until the meat is brown and drain off the excess fat.

4. Add the peppers, onions and celery to the pan.

5. Add the diced tomatoes, tomato sauce, beef broth and coffee. Stir to combine.

6. Add the spices - cumin, chilli powder, garlic powder, onion powder, ground oregano, salt and black pepper.

7. Bring to a boil, reduce heat, cover and simmer for 1.5 to 2 hours.

Paleo and Keto

Paleo- Decorate with sliced avocado, onions and / or chopped fresh parsley.

Keto / low carb: Decorate with sour cream, cheese and / or avocado slices.

Slow Cooking Mode:

1. In a large pan melt butter over medium heat. Add the chopped peppers, onion and celery and fry for 5-7 minutes until tender. Put the vegetables in the pan and set it aside.

2. Add ground beef and ground Italian sausages. Brown the meat and drain off the excess fat.

3. Add roasted vegetables, roasted ground beef and slow-cooked Italian sausages.

4. Add the diced tomatoes, beef broth, tomato sauce and coffee. Stir to combine.

5. Add the spices - cumin, chilli powder, garlic powder, onion powder, ground oregano, salt and black pepper. Stir to combine.

6. Cook over low heat for 6-8 hours or at high temperature for 4-6 hours.

Total servings 8

NUTRITION (1 serving)

CALORIES	275
PROTEINS	31 g
FATS	18 g
CARBS	4 g

45. Asian Soup with Keto Chicken Meatballs

Ingredients

For chicken balls:

0.6 lb. chopped chicken (270 g)

1 tablespoon chives (3 g), finely chopped

1 tablespoon fresh ginger (5 g), finely chopped

Season with salt and pepper

2 tablespoons of avocado oil (30 ml) for cooking meatballs

For the broth:

2.5 cups of chicken broth (600 ml)

1 teaspoon fish sauce (5 ml)

2 green onions (10 g), sliced

5 slices of fresh ginger (5 g)

Manual

1. Mix the chopped chicken with chives and ginger and season with salt and pepper.

2. Make small balls, the size of a ping-pong ball and put them in the fridge while preparing the broth.

3. Pour the chicken broth into a saucepan and add fish sauce and ginger slices.

4. Bring to boil and reduce to low heat for 10-15 minutes.

5. Heat the olive oil in a pot and cook the chicken balls until golden brown.

6. Cook enough from inside and out.

7. Taste the broth and adjust it by cooking more (to concentrate the taste) or adding more fish sauce.

8. Filter and divide in two bowls. Put the cooked meatballs into the broth and spread on the spring onions.

Total servings 2

NUTRITION (1 serving)

CALORIES	299
PROTEINS	23 g
FATS	26g
CARBS	3 g

46. Broccoli soup

Ingredients:

1-2 broccoli heads (including stems)

3 tablespoons of ghee or oil

1 small onion

5 cloves of garlic

1 teaspoon oregano

½ teaspoon parsley

1 teaspoon sage

1 teaspoon salt and pepper

1/4 teaspoon ginger

5-6 cups of vegetable stock or broth

4 teaspoons of butter

Manual:

1. Dice the onion and garlic.

2. Melt ghee in a saucepan over medium heat.

3. Add onions and garlic and stir. Add the spices and mix until the onions are almost translucent.

4. Cut the broccoli into equal pieces. Cut the stalk a little finer to cook well. Add the broccoli to the pan and cook for few minutes.

5. Add the vegetable stock to the pot and stir. Cover and cook, then reduce to low heat and simmer for about 20-30 minutes or until broccoli is tender.

6. The soup is best mixed with a hand blender. I like that and I love it, it makes cleaning so easy! You can also put it in a blender or food processor, but try to cool it down before mixing it in a blender.

7. Add the butter after mixing. This adds a delicious and creamy texture and taste. It is also always better to have vegetables with some kind of fat as it helps the body to absorb vitamins.

8. Add more butter, salt and pepper to your taste. I cooked mine with a little yogurt, but it would be just as good with a little sour cream.

Total servings 4

NUTRITION (1 serving)

CALORIES	215
PROTEINS	6 g
FATS	18g
CARBS	1 g

About Author

Talat Akhtar is the bestselling author of "Keto drinks".

Talat is an entrepreneur, motivational speaker, bodybuilder and an author.

She has competed in various bodybuilding competitions. She is a fitness expert.

Talat's primary focus, through her books is to help everyone around the world to become fit, healthy and live a happy life.

ONE LAST THING

If you really enjoyed this book or find it useful. I'd be really grateful if you write short review on Amazon. Your support really does make a difference and I read all your reviews personally. So I can get your feedback and make this book even better.

If you would like to leave a review all you have to do is go to amazon and type keto Soups by Talat Akhtar and leave a review.

Thanks a lot for your support.